THAT BOOK WRITTEN BY A TEACHER

My Bizarre Descent Into Exhaustion

Mrs D.M.

Dedicated to wine and the occasional packet of cheesy puffs.

Also dedicated to my wonderful family and friends.

That Book That Teacher Wrote
My Bizarre Descent Into Exhaustion

Introduction

This is the story of THAT side of my life, the blunders and screw ups and some of the reasons that I ended up choosing teaching as my turbulent bedfellow of a job. Also, perhaps the reasons I have stuck with it, Stockholm syndrome style, for the last 25 or so years. It isn't a warning or an endorsement and I don't think there's a moral. (OK, it's probably a warning) but the bizarre range of experience I have had has been quite a journey, sprinkled with more than the odd nugget of comedy and tragedy. If you think teaching is just one round of holidays after another I am here to dispel the myths, and to suggest that 6 weeks is the minimum amount of time it takes to recover from a 'nervous' breakdown.. this may not be coincidental. This book will give you an idea of what the job has been like for me.

It all came to a head one morning. The sunlight was forcing its way around the edge of the blind and into my bedroom as I woke up, and because of this I knew it must be the weekend. The rest of the week I stumbled from the house in the darkness, spent the day under florescent lighting in the company of disgruntled teenagers and dragged myself back home in the darkness once more. I became a commuting mole trained to run around a hamster wheel while being pulled in different directions, and weirdly, I became pretty good at it.

On the morning of Enlightenment, I had worked out it was the weekend. Then, in my brain there was nothing. I could not remember who I was or where I lived. I could not figure out which of my lives I was currently living, or what phase of life I was at. I could not remember who was lying next to me and whether or not I had children. Then, in a split second I remembered it all- my youth was gone, I was at the downhill end of my 40's and the heavy responsibilities of all the adult nonsense from the last few decades flooded in. The carefree, rebellious and principled person I was in my youth was almost worn away, trapped and silenced in a tired face and the relentless timetable of adultness. I was now going grey, a weary mum to four almost adult people, working hard in a challenging job and watching the years slip by, hurtling towards decrepitude and darkness. I had been so full of energy- where was that 16-year-old, fuelled illegally by pints of snakebite and black, who had swayed down the middle of the road on the way back from the village pub joyously singing 'Tie Me Kangaroo Down Sport' with a random Australian house guest?

After a steaming turd of a year, and following my confused awakening that weekend I decided that it was time to look back and figure out what I've been doing. If I live to be 96 it means I am currently middle aged, and this seems like a good time to reflect, (although I still wonder what I want to do when I grow up). How did I get myself into this position? To answer this question, I have zoomed right back to the 1970's, to my childhood. I have skipped some of the more personal or tedious stuff, (or have I?) to look at what has influenced me. It's a question we can all ask ourselves and because we are told that we all have a book inside us, I decided it was time to get that book out, however uncomfortable the birthing process and however ugly this baby turns out to be.

Chapter 1 Kiss, Cuddle and Torture

As a child I spent many long and happy hours being Wonder Woman. I would enthusiastically spin round on the spot, trying to trap people with my (imaginary) golden lasso and force them into my personal space. Nothing much has changed; this pretty much sums up the decades that I've spent teaching. Whether it's been primary, early years, secondary, mainstream, independent or additional/special needs, if you have enthusiasm, hope and magic, or at least a good imagination, and if you can trap people for long enough, the theory is that you might be able to help them…

When I was at school, Wonder Woman and rolling down hills were the obvious playtime choices for me, but there were other games- playing Batman and Robin was popular, however, roles were limited as the only boy in the school called Robin always got that part and we all hated him a bit for it. He had no flying or jumping skills, not enough specialist knowledge of the Batcave or Batmobile and never put much effort in- just the odd half hearted 'Pow' or feeble air punch. Having a female Batman would have been ridiculous, so the girls at my primary school did lots of handstands instead and pretended to be offended if people saw their pants.

Another favourite game of ours was 'Kiss, cuddle and torture' and this one was probably the best in terms of preparing us for the future, or 'Preparation for Adulthood', which is now the latest buzz phrase in curriculum planning. Somebody would be chosen to be the scary obsessive stalker type (I don't remember what we called them, but that was the job description) they would hunt down their victim until they had been caught and then give them the choice of 'kiss, cuddle or torture.' Torture was usually a Chinese burn- why twisting somebody's forearm was associated with China I have no idea, but looking back to the 70's there were lots of xenophobic shenanigans going on all the time. To some extent though, the game prepared me for my future marriage and later divorce, so it wasn't a complete waste of time.

I liked school in those days, and if you ignore all the odd stuff, it seemed as though they had got some of their priorities right. We had hot chocolate and rock buns when we came back into the hall after playing in the snow (imagine the risk assessments for that scenario now- slipping, hypothermia, death, scalding, choking, lactose intolerance) and a 'nature table' where we could deposit the curiosities we'd found when traipsing out and about (dirt, poo, germs, contamination, Avian flu, corona virus).

I thought I'd hit the jackpot one morning when I kidnapped a beautiful snail on my walk to school. This perfect snail was going to fulfil the criteria of the 'letter' table that week (things beginning with S) and make a pretty cool impact on the nature table too. I was justifiably excited, but my teacher didn't share my enthusiasm and completely freaked out, shouting and demanding I take my gorgeous gastropod out of her sight. My lovely snail had to go and relocate, dumped on the barren tarmac of the yard without even the briefest sliming of the nature table. I still think of that snail fondly, even now. Recently I was discussing this with a friend and she confessed to taking her gran's false teeth in to school for the nature table. It seemed her teacher had been more tolerant than mine and the teeth had sat there happily grinning all day, while her gran had been furiously searching for them. My friend shrugged and said that at the time she hadn't seen the problem, as there was always the spare pair she kept for best.

Generally, though, school made us want to learn,

made us desperate to go out and discover things, something which we seem to destroy so easily these days once formal education and all its traps, tests and pitfalls begin. At school we learned about local plants and animals, took owl pellets apart to see the miniscule bones inside them and even as infants we could identify different leaves and seeds. We were taught to respect the countryside, to understand the rhythms and the life cycles happening in nature regardless of whatever humans were up to. If we teach young children about their environment they will grow up to love and protect it, which is why playing outside is so important.

At home this curiosity continued- my brother and I would often catch creatures from the river and release them into the pond in the back garden. We had newts, goldfish, water snails and all sorts of interesting things living in there, or deposited in there as an experiment. My younger cousin came to visit one day and plonked Tom the tortoise into this watery habitat too. This wasn't good news for Tom as he sank like a stone, and despite us rushing to rescue him, he was never quite himself after that. In fact, he wasn't himself every year, as mum would force him into hibernation in the freezer and the tortoise would inevitably wake up dead in the spring.

She decided in the early 1980's to buy a Great African Bullfrog tadpole, to spice up the pond. Its head was as big as an egg and it had evil squinty little tadpole eyes. I think she also felt obliged to buy it because I went through an awkward phase of fainting in shops, so we ended up with extra stuff that we didn't need to make up for the inconvenience of having me on their floor. I woke up near the doorway of our local Spar shop once, looking up at the freezer, and we enjoyed a lot of Vienetta that week. I must have done the pet shop a few times as we got the bullfrog and collected a cupboard full of good quality hamster bedding, even though the hamster changed even more frequently than the tortoise. The impact of Bull Frogs on our native pond life wasn't considered until years later and then their importation was rightly banned. After its release we were never sure whether it had survived or whether the pond was just going through a lean patch. Years later my dad found it's dead froggy body, a terrifying Jabba the Hutt of a creature, sitting menacingly overlooking its domain.

Usually, if things were still alive, but peaky, my parents gave them a nip of whisky, or applied it to the ailment. When the hamster decided to check out the ash pan while the fire was lit, he was put in a little saucer of whisky to heal his tiny feet and to help him with the shock. Recently my stepmother reminisced about visiting my dad while they were 'courting' and told us of her surprise when she had discovered a poorly carp in the kitchen sink, swimming in diluted whisky. The remedy never had a good success rate, but because it would be rude to let the animals drink alone they always joined them in a little tipple and drank to their good health, which made the humans feel better at least. One of the hamsters had awesome escape skills and a liking for the inside of the old piano we had been given, so it would climb inside and run along the pegs attached to the keys. If you bear in mind the family link with the local spiritualist church (more detail on that later) you could imagine why the random plinking and plonking of piano keys sent nervous visitors running and made little Tiggy into a legend, at least to my brother and I.

We used to go on caravanning holidays to Devon, and our regular walk to the pub for scampy or jumbo sausage and chips in a basket took us through a graveyard which was littered with glow worms. It was amazing, every night I would hunt them down amongst the coloured grave chippings and collect them in a jam jar, every morning we would be repulsed by how creepy looking these crawlies were in the daylight. I went back and found the graveyard as an adult, waited till it was dark and excitedly looked for the little green lights.

There were none. I have carried the guilt of collecting those glow worms for decades now- single handedly wiping out probably the last little constellation of them in England. Looking back, maybe it would be fair to say our family had a love of nature but a limited understanding of what should live where and how to look after things...but then there was no Google, so if the adults didn't know what they were doing you were screwed.

Chapter 2 Whatever happened to Flashers?

With no phone or internet distractions, we all spent most of our time outside on bikes, playing football, fishing with nets or riding the 'rapids' on lilos down by the river in the summer. We had the freedom to walk down to the River Wear from our house, accepting that on the way there would probably be a Flasher in a raincoat that we would have to run from. There was a dodgy bit where we crossed the railway line, if the Flasher was waiting at that point it was a dilemma which way to run. Could we make it home? Or would we get to the river? We were aware but unaware of the dangers of strangers and they weren't taken very seriously. To be honest, I probably wasn't much of a target anyway. I wore the hand me downs of the Yorkshire cousins who I have never seen or heard of since, and my brother's cast-offs. Picture the scene- red satin Starsky and Hutch bomber jacket (which was unisex I think- or maybe I'm kidding myself, it could have been just for boys) my dad's oversized deerstalker hat with the earflaps tied under my chin and a pair of my brother's old brown flared cords. Often these would be accessorised by red, white and blue knee AND elbow pads, which were probably bought at some point in celebration of the Queen's silver jubilee, along with a snake belt and probably a set of braces. If I remember rightly all sorts of items were linked to Her Majesty in the late 1970's and I wonder how many of them she secretly wore herself.

The protection of the padding was vital if I decided to sew myself into my pair of lethal metal roller-skates, which were, even then, recognised as being stupidly dangerous. I certainly couldn't be victim blamed for encouraging those Flashers to flash. At about this time my mother thought it was hilarious to tell my brother and I that she had written to 'Jimllfixit' to ask him if we could be a pantomime horse, I was to be the rear end. There had been no consultation on this- I'd never expressed any interest in being the back end of any sort of animal but this was typical of my mum's sense of humour. I was such a dozy child that every week I watched the programme from behind the green velour sofa, in real terror in case I was on it.

In those days, girls wore long white socks with holes in them and I was shaken daily by my teacher Mrs Smack-bottom Fletcher and told that it was time I pulled them up. This was confusing to me as my socks were usually up and I couldn't tell the time. I annoyed her even more one day by stealing all the tiny little wooden animals from the reception class and hiding them in my socks. They were irresistible, tiny white ducks, tiny yellow chicks... Looking back, I think it was the chicks that drew me in but once they were in my socks I couldn't stop. I think I left some of the larger animals to fend for themselves, but I did have quite an uncomfortable-even disabling collection in there without them. This urge to collect things and store them in undergarments was passed on in my genes to my younger daughter. She stole all the decorations from the bottom half of the Christmas tree at nursery and hid them in her pants. Her accomplice and her were obviously spotted by the staff, who watched for some time with amusement and amazement. One of the items was a large star, which made it difficult for her to walk, but she was a determined little thing and boldly continued to fill her pants with every last reachable bauble. History had repeated itself, as apparently it does sometimes.

As soon as I saw my mum at the end of the day, she spotted my stash of stolen animals poking horizontally out from all the holes and I was in big trouble. The next day I had to admit my evil deed to the teacher and give them all back. I'd only stolen them because I felt sorry for them being at school all night alone, but Smack-bottom Fletcher wasn't impressed by that sort of sentimental weakness, so she shook me even more, presumably trying to shake all the badness out. If I develop dementia, I think she might be to blame. Or I might blame my older brother David who took it as his mission in life to inflict head injuries on me. In his defence, I was easily led. Some of my injuries were my own fault for following his instructions ('see what happens if you wiggle your handlebars while riding downhill as fast as you can' 'see what happens if you attach some string to that heavy thing and pull it' 'see what happens if you jump down all the stairs')

Looking back I don't think he liked me much. He took command of the lego and mechano while I was left trying to create sophisticated cityscapes and ground-breaking feats of engineering from stickle bricks and floppy fuzzy felt. He developed a convoluted library system for our small collection of Mr Men and Enid Blyton books which made it impossible for me to borrow any of them to read, I had to crack the Enigma code first. He had the cool Chopper while he convinced my parents that what I really needed was the most embarrassingly uncool old ladies folding bike, parts of which tended to fold themselves up as I was riding along.

Alan, the driving instructor he recommended when I reached 17 had a moving toupee which was very distracting. Every time I got in the car his hair would be travelling in a different direction and I had a phobia of doing emergency stops in case it flew off and landed on my lap. My brother would be amused every time he saw I had a driving lesson and waved me off cheerfully. This was typical of the kind of annoying recommendation he would give. Once he even convinced me that the suet in sweet mince was marzipan so I spent ages fishing out all the little lardy sausages and gobbling them up quick smart before he got a chance. When he told me I had eaten suet I threw up- not successfully as the lard had merely formed a thick coat on the insides of my mouth and very little of it had made its way to my stomach.

I was an annoying child, I daydreamed a lot, did a lot of spinning round and liked creepy crawlies, and of course I had a history of stealing farm animals. I'm not sure if Smack-Bottom Fletcher hated me or all children, or maybe she was doing that thing where teachers are told in training not to smile till Christmas. I remember her as the old witch from Hansel and Gretel, fattening children up on the sly, ready to eat them, but she was probably only 30ish at the time and probably wasn't even a cannibal. Other teachers were more sympathetic, but I don't remember their names. I remember odd things, like the mother of pearl earrings one of them wore and a male teacher who threw the board rubber randomly and shouted when there was no need, although he did let the least annoying of us bang the chalk off it on the wall at break time. As I moved through the school system and changed schools, it became clear that I shouldn't be thinking of doing any sort of job that involved maths (which is ironic, because I did). My dad tried his best to help me but I exasperated him and it always ended up with me screaming in the downstairs toilet. When I was older, we had to suffer the school Hunger Games of mental arithmetic. The losers (who had any remnants of logic panicked out of their brains by the stress) had to stand on their chairs and were somehow looked down on by the victorious people, still smugly sitting in the same place where they had started the lesson. Humiliation and punishment were the way teachers operated sometimes, so it is no surprise that many adults now hate them and have passed on their hatred to their children and grandchildren who are now difficult to help. I strongly suspect that the current Secretary of State for Education is one of these people.

I was lucky, however, I had a human English teacher. She would flout the rules of normal teacher behaviour by sitting on the tables while she talked, and sometimes she would laugh. She saw me as a person and when my parents split up during my GCSEs she asked after me, as a person.

Chapter 3 Normal Person to Teacher

I was briefly a normal adult and a non-teacher after I graduated. I messed about for a bit being a promotion assistant for the local newspaper in Lancaster, which wasn't as glamorous as it sounds and then worked in the newspaper office doing classified ads. The promotion assistant role mainly involved standing in supermarkets wearing a stupid costume or unflattering t shirt and trying to give free newspapers away. It was dull and very badly paid. I spent a lot of time 'people watching' and found it sad to notice the same elderly people come in to buy their daily handful of lottery tickets, the hope fading from their faces like that scene in Charlie and the Chocolate Factory where the wrapper is opened and there is no golden ticket. I now fear I am going to become one of those old people as the temptation to enter the Euro millions for the £127,000,000 is too much to resist. I wasn't good at the promotions job and could only be enthusiastic about the newspapers for the first hour or so, when I knew the manager was watching. I was told off for lolloping about and sometimes admit I had to dump the newspapers in a bin when the boredom was too much. It did, however, make me aware of how suspicious I naturally appear to other people, and that is something I still have to work on. Many people would swerve away from me, even if the paper was free and I was offering them a chocolate bar or complementary holiday to Barbados to go with it.

When the classified Ads job came up, I went for it, and although the salary was terrible it was better than the £20 a day I'd been earning as a promotion assistant. The interview was conducted by a very smart and earnest young man called Gavin who drove some kind of yellow Japanese sports car. I think it was meant to impress people, but I have a 'car blindness' thing where almost all cars look the same, so it was lost on me. Gavin took his job extremely seriously and I remember him asking me where I wanted to be in five years. Back then this was a bog standard interview question, along with 'Do you want children?', a question which would now trigger an inquiry into discrimination of protected characteristics. It struck me that five years on I probably wouldn't want to be there, doing that job, with him, but I kept quiet and muttered something about having a great dog, and maybe wanting another. He nodded sagely, as though talking about dogs was fine, and it looked as though nobody had prepared him for what to do when your candidate answers a question. In fact, it was similar to when

I once had to speak French to a pharmacist (in France) to explain that my daughter had been stung and had suffered an allergic reaction. The intimidatingly crisp and clean looking lady smiled, a little patronisingly I thought, and started answering at full speed. I had forgotten that I would understand nothing of her reply, so I just smiled blankly and apologetically until she figured out how to answer me in English. I suspect she could smell my my GCSE French a mile off.

For that year working for the Garstang courier I enjoyed the simple things in life, such as having a wee when I needed to (I may be embracing that again in the coming years- I have seen the adverts and apparently nobody can even tell!). Having lunchbreaks with other adults (rather than with children or teenagers whose disgusting habits put you off eating.) I also took full advantage of the joy of the slightly padded spinny round chair, of drinking coffee while it's hot, although I once tried to do both together and nearly broke the keyboard. Plus of course, going home knowing you had finished your day's work and nothing more needed to be done. There was all manner of adult hobbies, it was fantastic.

The job itself and the necessity to do paperwork distracted from these perks though, and I found the traditional sexism of the newspaper boss and the other big cheeses annoying. After spilling my coffee on the keyboard while spinning round once too many times, I decided I needed to think seriously about what I was doing with my life. My self- destructive nature wanted more, I decided I wanted a career where I could 'give something back'. In theory I quite liked the children I had met (although looking back to that time I don't think I'd met any real ones) and of course I remember mistakenly thinking that teaching was a respectable and worthy thing to do.

I completed my PGCE in west Cumbria, as my then husband was finishing his degree at Preston. I presumed the catchment area would be nice, with polite country children who wore Cath Kidston (or similar wholesomely branded) wellies, enjoyed a ramble in the hills and knew a thing or two about sheep. I was looking forward to renting a cosy stone cottage with a log fire and spending weekends climbing mountains.

The reality of affordable rented houses was hugely different. We ended up in an estate of ugly 70's bungalows, and ours had original ugly fixtures (these would be highly sought after 'retro features' now) including offensive carpets, weird metal bathroom tiles, doors with multiple panels of wobbly non-safety glass, a stinky boiler and a monkey puzzle tree. I was very wrong about the catchment area too, back then Maryport and Whitehaven were economically deprived and many of the people were struggling. In my first placement in Workington we found that the school field was out of action for weeks while all the topsoil was removed with a JCB- someone had planted a load of hypodermic syringes in the field, with their needles pointing upwards. The children were often streetwise and lived with parents on the run from debts and other troubles in the northeast.

This first school placement was in Workington, the school was an old Victorian building, with high ceilings long windows and patches of damp and fungus. The staff were helpful and eventually even friendly to us, once you got past the abrasive Cumbrian sense of humour. Half of the people on the PGCE were male, which we were told was unusual. At that time most teachers were female but 90% of head teachers were male, so the chances of female teachers becoming heads was slim. This didn't bother me much, as I wasn't intending to become a head anyway, I just wanted to be a good teacher and that seemed to be tricky enough. There was much more to the job than I'd imagined, and I had thought that having lived with my mother, who was a teacher, I would have had more insight than most. The irony is that my eldest daughter who has always been intolerant of my 'moaning' about my job is now doing a PGCE. I think it's been enlightening for her as all she seems to do is moan.

This was the mid 1990's and Sellafield, (which out

of interest was the world's first commercial power plant and one of Europe's foremost nuclear reprocessing plants), had decided to try to soften its image, reach out to the community and offer free school trips to their newly created wildlife 'reserve.' The visitors centre had benefitted from a multi-million-pound refurbishment so the school I was placed with took advantage of the offer and we went off for the day to explore the reserve. Worksheets were also provided and attached self-importantly to clip boards- we were wildlife spotting. Given a couple more decades this might have been more successful, but it was bleak when we went, the trees were just seedlings and the ponds were empty. There was literally no wildlife to be found, nothing. Perhaps somebody had bought a bulk load of great African bull frogs to kick start the excitement and it had backfired... or maybe all the jokes about radioactivity and their strange effects on wildlife had some truth in them. Despite this, the children enjoyed the bus ride and their packed lunches, and most school trips are spent going to the toilet and back anyway.

The lessons we prepared back then needed real effort and time to be engaging. Being faced for the first time with a group of children and knowing I had to somehow teach them something was scary. In the beginning, we were caught up with the delivery of lessons and learning how to manage behaviour. Children and young people can smell weakness or lack of confidence and they act like a pack, one or two bringing you down and the rest hungrily waiting for the kill, baying for your blood. Survival was the real objective of every lesson, despite what was written on the blackboard. The realisation that teaching and learning are two distinct aspects of a lesson came later, in the beginning we just hoped for the best as we launched into presenting.

We followed the national curriculum document, decided upon our own way of teaching a topic and then created all the resources to go with it. There was nothing available to print off- no online teaching resources were available at all, no Twinkl or TES, everything came from your own imagination and relied on your creativity and motivation to deliver a good lesson. The only thing the newly invented internet could offer was an occasional hit from Wikipedia and even that couldn't be trusted as being factual. The school did however, allow us to borrow some ancient wooden letter templates to draw round so that our display headings were neat, and they gave us sticky back plastic to protect them with. I'm not even sure laminators were invented then as an alternative, as almost everything flat was covered in bubbly plastic, peeling and hairy at the edges. If you felt extravagant you could buy the odd teaching ideas book which contained photographs of other people's displays and an occasional worksheet, but they were expensive and not massively inspiring. Worksheets were all handwritten and records were kept in books or at the back of a huge planner. It was all very time consuming, and I remember spending a whole evening cutting around some small yellow cardboard feet for a lesson on coordinates. My tutor wisely asked what the point was when I could have used plastic counters instead, but time management comes with experience, and I didn't have much of that.

In my eagerness to become a proper adult, and after only a couple of months into the course, I started to think about how to get a job when it was finished. In the proactive style of my mother, and probably because she told me to, I wrote letters to several schools in Cumbria and County Durham. I did this the old-fashioned way, using a pen and a piece of paper, and I sent them through the post. I enquired if there were any vacancies and heard back from a small 'independent' school in a small rural village near where I had lived, they were looking for a year 5/6 teacher. This wasn't ideal as I really wanted a job in early years and was apprehensive about working out of mainstream education, but I knew it would be silly to turn down the possibility of a permanent contract. I attended a series of 'interviews' with the Head 'mistress' (yes- we still needed to have a gender attached to the job role although the title 'Sister' should have been a giveaway- that and the nun's habit) These interviews were like a cross between the final stages of The Apprentice and a social experiment. I was scrutinised heavily and repeatedly, my character was explored and my ability to handle a full cup of tea with a saucer was tested to the full. My new boss was diminutive, astute, quick witted, occasionally fiercesome, and yet she also exuded an aura of calmness and tranquillity. Luckily the topic of farm animal smuggling did not come up in the interview, but I felt she knew about it already anyway, that and all my other sins. There was no lesson observation, they took me on the basis of my references, interviews, manners and tea juggling abilities. I had secured my first job, in a Convent, with The Sisters of Mercy (not the band).

Chapter 4 The Convent

This was as surreal as it sounds but I embraced it, and even ditched my beloved Doc Martens to enter a world of dodgy teacher footwear I have never escaped from. The other stipulations (there were more than two when I think about it) was that back in 1997, a convent schoolteacher must always wear a skirt, this did not apply to the small smattering of male staff, although the Father who lived somewhere in the bowels of the building did wear a dress. The students wore a traditional brown and gold uniform, girls in skirts and boys in shorts, and the nuns wore navy blue. Staff were under cover and dressed as normal people, but if we saw a nun blending as a member of the public it felt really weird, especially if they were spotted out of hours in the local gym. We were also told to avoid bringing resources and stuff into school in carrier bags (I think that rule was added when I joined the staff and lowered the tone). One of the nuns had a Harrods carrier bag, which bizarrely she loved and could not be parted from, and this was the only exception.

The school had an interesting history and had been running for over a hundred years in a confusing and complicated stone building which had been extended a number of times. The front of the building had a lawn and a beautiful camellia tree with pink flowers. A narrow path led to a large black set of gates built into a high stone wall which ran alongside the path and on to the road, right in the middle of the village. The gate and the wall were apparently needed to stop the hot-blooded local youths from invading and deflowering the secondary school pupils, who were all girls.

A small group of nuns still lived in the convent, up a secret flight of stairs which led to their living quarters. A couple of the nuns still taught RE or languages, and some were retired but were still spotted fleetingly, gliding through the corridors, serenely carrying bowls of custard, never making a sound. I presumed they had a kitchen upstairs somewhere, but the pull of that school dinner custard was obviously too much for them to resist. There was a beautiful old chapel in the centre of the school, decorated with carved and polished dark wood and this was used each day for prayers and mass. Non catholic members of staff did not go into the chapel, so I did not see it until years later when a friend invited me to her daughter's christening there. When I started work at the convent, I soon found that I was nearer in age to my pupils than to my colleagues, but this was fine, they were all good humoured, helpful, friendly and could all still balance a cup of tea as well as anyone.

My classroom was the only teaching room at the top of the building and next to the nun's sleeping quarters, accessed via a rabbit warren of corridors and up a very narrow flight of stairs. Life sized effigies of the Virgin Mother in pale blue and white robes would look down upon us from wooden plinths stationed throughout the building. This helped to keep everyone in line, much in the same way that scarecrows in high viz jackets slow down speeding motorists. We had no computers in classrooms but there was a rolling blackboard which spun quite fast if you tried hard enough. In an empty classroom downstairs, there was a big grey square backed TV and a video cassette recorder from the 1980's attached to a tall stand with wheels, which could be booked if teachers really insisted on using modern technology.

I checked out the resources left behind by a previous teacher in a large and musty antique dark wood chiffonier, it had large double doors at the bottom with ornate brass handles and curved drawers above. On the top was a large oval mirror, the glass was spotty and dark with age. It wasn't even close to the kind of bright modern moulded classroom furniture which was available to buy in the YPO catalogue, but it had character. I found a dusty old book about science from the 1960's in which it was excitedly reported that 'in the future, space travel may be possible, man may even visit the moon'. I kept it as a history book rather than a science book.

It was exciting, a bit like travelling back through a time portal in one of those movies where you end up in an attic, exploring ancient manuscripts to find an answer. Other teaching resources were filled with grammar and punctuation exercises from decades ago- the scenarios used as examples were dry, outdated, sexist, racist and unnecessarily complicated. Having said that, the government's recent obsession with pointless and archaic grammar exercises means that some of those books might still have a role in helping young Kieran with his fronted adverbials.

The pupils' desks were the Victorian kind you can still see in Beamish Museum. They were individual wooden desks with hinged lift up lids, providing a sizeable storage area inside for exercise and text books (or for contraband snacks and wild creatures that would have been much happier living outside, as I was to discover later). There was a handy inkwell on the top and a deep groove for keeping the quills neat and tidy. The smell in the room was slightly foisty, a smell of history and religion, dedication and seriousness. This school bore no resemblance to any of my teaching placements, even the traditional little red stone school at Allenby next to the Sea had plastic desks and brightly coloured coat pegs.

Every time a saint's feast day was celebrated the nuns would open the 'parlour' at lunchtime, which was a large and austere sitting room opposite the staff room, and they would also open the wine. This was a frequent event, as there are at least eight super important Feast days each year and every day of the year is a special day for at least one Saint. The parlour was like a flashback to the 1940's, with faded back winged chairs, antimacassars and antique coffee tables. Around the room there were elderly plastic flower arrangements, the carpet was floral patterned and so were the wallpaper and curtains, though none of them complimented each other. There were a few paintings with a religious theme and a sizeable crucifix above the electric fire.

We would be expected to attend these events, which would always start with prayers and end up with refreshments. These included trays of salmon and cucumber or ham sandwiches, cut into fiddly little triangles and some sort of impossible to eat dessert designed to fall apart when touched, such as cheesecake or black forest gateaux. The social experiment would continue. How much wine was appropriate to drink on a saint's day? Did it depend on the saint? Or on what subjects were being taught in the afternoon? Would I safely make it up all those stairs to my classroom? Would the saints be offended if you refused in favour of the tea and saucer trial? It was a tricky route to navigate as a new teacher and I felt sure none of my PGCE contemporaries would be struggling with the same issues.

I had mainly been hired because they believed I could steer them safely through the brand-new introduction of key stage two SATS and ensure all the pupils left the primary department with excellent results. This was based on the fact that I had been trained using the new 'national curriculum' a phenomenon that none of the other staff had experienced and the curriculum which the SAT tests examined. As I had been trained using the documents, I couldn't understand what the alternative was, but the O Level or GCSE results were good, so they were certainly doing something right.

The school was unusual in that it catered for pupils of all academic abilities. It was a fee-paying school, but the fees were a fraction of the other independent schools in the area which led to an interesting mix of students. I wondered if some children attended the convent as a diagnosis of additional needs would be suggested in a mainstream school and some parents would want to avoid their child being 'labelled.' I would happily spend my lunchtimes giving pupils extra support and read as much as I could find about the 'gift' of dyslexia and other barriers to learning. The parents were an interesting mix too. As a clueless 23-year-old I was oblivious to the status some of them held, whether they were infamous criminals, famous racehorse trainers, farmers, or powerful local business owners, I had no idea. This was a good thing as I was easily intimidated and remember vividly my first solo parent's night when my first parent, a police officer, told me that he'd been told I was young, but he had no idea I would be 'THIS young'. How I wish I'd appreciated that comment instead of being insulted. Since my second year of teaching, I have looked at least 45, and I hold him partly responsible.

The school catered for children from nursery age to fifth year or year 11. I taught poetry to the infants while the nuns taught my class RE and I apprehensively stepped into the nursery once a week. I would cover secondary lessons if another teacher were absent, as we never used supply staff. We had no teaching assistants either as the job had not been invented then, but there were a couple of nursery nurses. I think one of the reasons that I feel guilty delegating jobs to support staff now is because I was trained to do it all myself, even if that meant being insanely overworked all the time and in a constant tizz. I have to say at this point that I've worked with dozens of amazing and incredibly gifted teaching assistants over the years, who work tirelessly for the children and staff they support.

After making initial assessments of my class, it was clear that there was a lot of national curriculum to cover before they sat the SATS, most of it, in fact.

The parents were paying for this and would expect the school to achieve a good ranking in the newly invented league tables. Some of the students would also remind me occasionally that their parents paid my salary, which was very endearing. I worked them hard, and I was relentlessly seeking progress and achievement. An independent schools' inspection recognised the acceleration of progress in my class, and I was praised for it, but I now know that just because I was good at teaching did not mean I was a good teacher. I was pushing them too hard, but we had had no training on additional needs or mental wellbeing and when I realised one of my form was plucking out her own eyebrows, I didn't really understand how stressed she was. I am ashamed to admit that, especially now I have a responsibility in my school for mental health. The pressure of the situation was building on me too, as some of the rest of the department continued happily arranging summer and winter fayres and allowing the serious stuff to happen in years 5 and 6. Now I have children of my own and a more balanced perspective I think that those children probably loved arranging fayres and the value or purpose of KS2 SATS is deeply flawed. We are in danger of setting them up to feel inadequate very early on and of completely killing the natural curiosity and creativity that leads to lifelong learning.

Light relief came at Christmas when I naively decided I could write amusing Christmas plays. I tried to use the strengths of the pupils in my class, the children who were good at singing sang, the dancers danced and those who had success in the 'Public Speaking Exams' narrated. Except for one girl who played the part of 'Christmas Past' in my blatant rip off of a Muppets Christmas Carol, she was just tall, and although she had lots of other talents, I felt I needed someone tall to walk slowly around the stage and point at far off things. Her mum spoke to me passive-aggressively afterwards and told me how disappointed she had been not to have a speaking part, and I felt very guilty. I think she belonged to a different cohort to the one with the girl who was plucking out her own eyebrows but that didn't make it any better. My plays accidentally became even more offensive because my knowledge of the Catholic faith was sketchy at best. The following year I took the (apparently deeply religious) song 'The Twelve Days of Christmas' and exchanged all the things in the song for what I considered to be other more interesting items, including slugs and 'Frenchmen' which was also probably very inappropriate. My comedy heroes at the time were Vic Reeves and Bob Mortimer so you can imagine how it was. The head teacher took me to one side afterwards and gently asked me if I would like to choose a published play for my class to perform next time.

After a few weeks into the job, I got the hang of assemblies, which was an achievement as the prayers rolled on straight from one to the next and I was expected to lead them. All the Primary and nursery children would gather in the gym and the primary staff would station themselves around the outside, expectantly looking at whoever was leading the assembly to set the ball rolling. They began;

'Oh My God, I give to you, all the things I say and do, all my work and all my happy play, I will give to God today, Father in Heaven I give you today, all that I think, and do, and say.'

I wasn't entirely comfortable with putting forward the idea that God could see what people were thinking- my brother had told me this when I was a child and it had caused a lot of confusion. It meant that whatever he did, I wasn't even able to privately think bad thoughts about him, he literally controlled my mind.

This prayer led to the Hail Mary, which brought an even more melancholy tone to the assembly.

'Hail Mary, full of grace, the Lord is with thee, blessed art thou amongst women, and blessed is the fruit of thy womb Jesus. Holy Mary, Mother of God, pray for us sinners, now and at the hour of our death, Amen.'

This was followed by the Lord's Prayer and some additional seasonal or targeted prayers. The only way I could remember the order was that the first one started with the words 'Oh My God' and I always thought how appropriate that phrase was, when I looked out on to a sea of brown uniforms all waiting to tell me that their parents paid my salary, I was too young for this job and they didn't like what I was doing to people's eyebrows.

Chapter 5 Gregory Peck

It was during one of these lengthy prayer sessions a couple of years into the job that I fainted, and woke up in the arms of Sister A. When I immediately threw up enthusiastically all over her, in front of the entire primary school, she knew the score. My first-born child was starting to make her presence felt. Sister A was worldly wise, had a wicked sense of humour and was the lady with a totally inappropriate love of Harrods. Sister A's second love was for Gregory Peck, and she liked to retell the story of how The Lord had taught her a valuable lesson about keeping her worldly desires in check.

She had accidentally become distracted watching Gregory on the TV, and this had made her late for a hair appointment. She had hurriedly got changed into a clean habit and rushed out of the convent, anxious that she was keeping the hairdresser waiting. She was caught in various well-meaning conversations as she made her way through the village which had delayed her even further. On her way back to the convent, she had felt a draft up the back of her legs and once inside, she realised to her horror that because Gregory had distracted her, she had accidentally tucked her habit into the back of her knickers. Instead of dwelling on her embarrassment and considering how many of the people she had spoken to had seen her pants she simply looked up and said, "Nice one, Lord".

On another occasion she had left a collection box in the shop where her sister worked (her real sister) so that people could donate to the leper charity which the convent supported. Her sister had misheard and had told every customer that the convent was raising money for 'The lesbians', which sister A thought was hilarious, and happily a great deal of money was raised.

In an effort to please the nuns and cause minimal disruption to my class I took only a few weeks maternity leave and even arranged for qualified family members to cover many of my lessons. Between them, I had English, maths and science covered. As soon as I could, I went back to school and taught, with my tiny newborn daughter hunched in her car seat at the back of the classroom. It was almost SAT time, and I believed that the tests took priority- my teaching job was the most important thing going on. This is the problem with teachers, we get so involved with our school family that our own family takes second place and we often mistakenly believe that we are irreplaceable.

When she was just a few weeks old, I handed her to the most amazing childminder ever, Judith, to be looked after full time. I knew she would be well cared for, her kitchen was always full of sunshine, wholesome food and things to glue and stick (in an orderly fashion and according to agreed boundaries), and she was excellent at routines, something which I struggled with. I expressed pints of milk at break time, sitting on the edge of an immaculate single bed in one of the small and tidy convent bedrooms, which admittedly felt like a very odd thing to do. I then put my homemade milk in the staff-room fridge and took it with me at the end of the day, freezing the surplus in ice cube trays to give to the lovely childminder. I didn't realise until years later that she had been repulsed by my breast milk, and had always binned it and bought large tubs of powdered SMA instead.

At lunchtimes I would try to escape and give her a feed and like many new mums, I found adapting to full time work and motherhood emotionally draining. I was also a bit fat and depressed, couldn't fit into my pre-baby clothes and had no opportunity to buy any alternatives. That continued for about ten years, as online shopping wasn't a thing and for a number of reasons it always seemed impossible to go clothes shopping. Most of my clothes were donated from family members and my own clothes were a weird mixture of old student stuff (massive woolly rainbow jumpers and dungarees) too-small corporate newspaper job stuff and too-small super respectable convent stuff, most of which was stained with big breast milk chromatography circles. I started to lose myself at this point in my motherhood adventure and I remember being really stressed by having to cobble together a set of white clothes so I could take part in an 'Eco project' with my class. It had been organised by local artists and was going to culminate in a Rio De Janeiro style carnival through the streets of our little village. We were all to wear white so as not to distract from the massive brightly coloured paper mache things that we had made. My white clothes (I don't ever remember buying any white clothes so they must have been beige) were too snug and I was dreading it, I should have still been on maternity leave but instead there I was, leaking, sleep deprived, feeling socially unacceptable and confused.

We collected in the lower school building of the local comprehensive school for a couple of days beforehand, the vast parquet floor was covered in sheets and piles of wire, wood, paper, paint and glue. On the first day we worked in teams with other schools creating the framework for the creations and on the second day we started to add the paper and the latex glue. I had my secret suspicions about whether or not I had a latex allergy, but this was work, and apart from wearing some latex gloves to protect me from the latex glue there wasn't much I could do. Very soon I seemed to be covered in the glue and the itching and hives began. My hands were swelling up to monstrous proportions and resembled a couple of neon inflatable pool toys or those big pointy hands Americans wear at baseball games. The hives were spreading and my asthma was starting to play up, my next symptom was a migraine, with blind spots. At this point I thought I should probably tell somebody and looking back I think it was the right thing to do. I went home, had a few anti-histamine tablets and some puffs of my inhaler and went to bed. Thankfully, or not, I recovered in time to take part in the mortifying prance through the village, in my tight white clothes. I have a feeling they let me bang a tambourine instead of holding the latex eco monster, but the memory is hazy and clouded by embarrassment.

I didn't like taking time off for illness or babies and at this time part time teaching work was unheard of and something you weren't entitled to ask for or expect. Eventually, after my physical and mental health started to suffer, and with a heavy heart, I resigned from The Sisters of Mercy. The following year the convent closed and locally it was the end of an era, a little bubble which had been lost in time was then gone forever. The buildings were made into flats and houses and the staff and pupils dispersed into other schools. I 'went on supply' which was nothing to do with drug dealing or arms trading.

Chapter 6 The Stresses of Small People

A year or so later I was pregnant with my second daughter, and shortly after she was born my older child became seriously ill. Over the course of a weekend, she almost faded away. She was drinking non-stop, weeing all the time, being sick and had no energy at all. Her weight had dropped to almost the same as her baby sister, her belly was distended but her arms and legs looked like little sticks and she had hollows above her ears, just like the photographs of the famine victims in Ethiopia in the 1980's. Her eyes were big dull saucers of darkness, and her blonde hair was thin and lank.

One of my closest friends suggested she had diabetes, as luckily for us her dog had the condition, and she recognised the symptoms. Her black lab cross 'Magic' had been drinking non-stop and weeing day and night and there were definite parallels. Eventually she was tested, but only after a fight with local health professionals who thought the idea was preposterous. We were sent straight to hospital where, after a little blip when a nurse kindly gave her some full sugar squash, we met the amazing consultant who was to look after her for the whole of her childhood. This man was kind, calm and reassuring and cared deeply about his patients. After her first shot of insulin, it was like watching a miracle happen in front of our eyes. She seemed to wake up, her appetite returned immediately and she ate a whole plate of hospital food, including the side salad.

The dawning of what was involved in caring for a toddler with diabetes was immense, it was like a tide of grief, the understanding that we could never be spontaneous again, everywhere we went we needed insulin, glucose, a blood tester, a finger pricker and test strips. Every time she looked tired, or was grumpy, or threw a tantrum, she had her blood tested. Every night I would wake at 2 am to test the blood from her little toes to check she was OK, and almost 20 years later I still have the same disturbed sleep pattern. All her food needed calculating for carbs, I read every label, weighed everything on special laptop type scales (which did the calculations for you- handy if you have them handy), and was super careful about everything she ate. It was far from easy. At that time, she was only just 3, and the only treatment was multiple injections of fast acting insulin, plus morning and night injections of long-acting insulin. Every time she ate, she needed an injection, with extra doses needed in times of sickness, growth, hot weather, stress or if well-meaning adults slipped her a lolly or bakewell tart. If the balance was wrong, she would have a hypo, and eventually we could see the signs -her nose would go pale, she would talk nonsense and have no energy to move. Sometimes it was impossible to see a pattern, despite keeping detailed records. If she was hyper, she had too much sugar in her system and would need an injection. At these times she acted as though she had drunk six pints, she was loud and cheeky, but unlike a drunk person, her breath smelled like peardrops, which was nice.

My flexible working arrangement was now essential as school staff were at that time strongly advised by the unions against giving insulin injections to pupils, which is understandable as if you get the dose even half a drop wrong it is not good news. Luckily for us, our local nursery was staffed by the most amazing team, one of them was a beautiful lady with crazily curly hair who wore sandals all year round, the only difference between summer and winter being the rainbow-coloured socks with built in toes that she reluctantly wore when it snowed. This lady, a fabulous force of nature, had the same condition and was more than happy to help. The school also accepted me as a supply teacher, and I made links with other local schools which fitted well with looking after my daughters.

I am still close friends with the team who worked in the nursery- all fantastic people. I learned a great deal from them, the inspirational teacher in charge went on to advise in early years and ultimately became an educational consultant. When you entered that nursery the atmosphere was relaxed, welcoming, busy and full of laughter. It was lovely to see a team work together so expertly. Each staff member was equal, there was no hierarchy and no need for egos. Long after the children had grown up the staff would reminisce about their nursery antics; each child was remembered with affection. I have my own memories of doing supply in that nursery, and two stand out.

One was an occasion when a small girl had been playing in the dressing up area, trying on hats, wings, beards and beads and had somehow managed to clasp an oversized purse on to her bottom lip. It was one of those old-fashioned metal clasps with two bobbles that snap together when it is closed. She screamed, a blood curdling, shrill and unforgettable sound (although her voice was slightly muffled by the size of the purse) and there was blood everywhere. It was a horrific scene, but eventually we unclamped her bottom lip, and she was released. She is all grown up now and I have heard that she suffered no long-term scars of any sort.

The other lasting memory I have was of my first

visit from the 'piano lady', a respectable Women's Institute sort of a lady who wore long pleated skirts and matching woollens. All the children were shepherded into the cosy story corner and settled happily on the multi coloured floor cushions around the piano. There was a ripple of excitement and whispers as she bustled in, as there usually is when a visitor comes into school. She settled herself, adjusted her spectacles and prepared her music, and the children were soon hushed and expectantly gazing at her, waiting for her to start playing. She started cheerfully plinking the opening lines of a nursery rhyme and in that moment all the little faces looked from her to me -to lead the singing. I realised with horror that I couldn't mime myself out of this one like I usually did in assemblies (I admit I have done this all my life). I was unexpectedly embarking on my first solo performance, and it was awful. I have never been any good at singing. I joined the choir at secondary school but after we had sung only one song the teacher lined us all up and demanded we sing solos until she rooted me out and asked me to leave. Back in the nursery, the piano teacher looked at me in genuine shock, as if I was the worst singer she had ever heard, and the children looked confused and a little scared. I'm sure one or two even started to cry.

From leaving the convent until a number of years later I worked supply in local schools including the schools that my eldest attended, so that I was nearby in case I was needed to give insulin injections or deal with other emergencies. I also took advantage of a government scheme running at the time which allowed teachers with five years' experience to do an open university course for free, so I did a post graduate diploma in child development. The aim was to do a psychology degree and then to train as an educational psychologist but the training for it in those days took several years and it wasn't something I could pursue, so the diploma amounted to the first year of the degree. Because of this interest, I was unexpectedly offered a job working with The Psychology Service and Oxford University collecting data to test if supplements of fish oil could improve learning. It was fascinating and the research took place in over 20 local primary schools. This meant I had the freedom to arrange appointments which fitted with family life, and I was once again able to reclaim some of my basic human rights (such as having a wee when I wanted to and getting a break to eat lunch.)

The selected children were given hobnobs laced with fish oil every day for a number of months to increase their intake of omega 3 and omega 6, which in theory would help the electrical impulses in their brains to move across the synapses more easily and so improve learning. These spiked hobnobs were disgusting and the regular feeding schedule may have added to the childhood obesity problem, but we weren't researching that (I'm pretty sure their hair was glossier and their noses shinier too- but we weren't researching that either.) It was my job to visit the schools and conduct a range of tests with the pupils, including reading and psychometric tests which involved little flip charts with black and white patterns and shapes which tested things like problem solving and spacial awareness. I enjoyed the flexibility of the job and visiting so many different schools was really interesting. Unfortunately, my childcare arrangements had to change, I needed to look after my eldest child again and had to leave the project. The research did show improvements in learning, but it was ultimately discredited – I never found out why (I suspected it was my fault for leaving the job and messing up the consistency of the data collection, another little thing that festers in the guilt box in my head, along with the extinct glow worms.)

After a few months of my eldest child being in the reception class, I reluctantly moved her from her first primary school. There were over 30 children in the class, which would be a large number of anything to look after all day- imagine 30 cats or 30 puppies, let alone 30 small humans who have been on the planet for about four years- just enough time to develop their personalities and follow their own agendas. Her teacher understandably found it impossible to keep an eye on her blood sugars and felt squeamish about the whole diabetes thing. She asked my daughter to test her blood in the toilets in case it upset the other children, which made her feel excluded and embarrassed. This was just as offensive to me as those people who think that breast feeding mums should feed their babies in the toilet, and for a few years I would take it as a personal challenge to breast feed one of her siblings while simultaneously giving her an insulin injection. I never had to defend myself though, nobody was that interested, and I was always discrete so it's doubtful if anyone even noticed. In her new school, classes were smaller, and the staff were again fabulous, compassionate, and understanding. I was thankful that I'd managed to convince them too that I was competent enough to employ on a supply basis and formed lasting friendships with this lovely new work family.

Chapter 7   A Mixed Bag

I taught in every year group and in schools all over the county but mainly in the same local schools. Being a supply teacher has its ups and downs. Schools who use supply agencies often do so because they find it tricky to secure the same regular staff, and it can be a sign that there are issues. Sometimes a class teacher has gone off with stress because the class are so difficult to cope with day in, day out, and the pupils then become used to a constant stream of different teachers, which just makes behavioural problems worse. 'Nice' schools usually retain their supply staff because they make them feel valued and part of the team, and they recognise the importance of building relationships. I became more skilled by doing supply, eventually I wasn't even fazed by being asked to teach ratio and probability to a lively year 6 class whose favourite sport was winding up supply teachers. It is more difficult, however, to maintain discipline and build relationships in a supply teacher role when you don't know the children's names. Even if they tell you their name it isn't necessarily their real name, (another example of 'Preparation for Adulthood' in action). I remembered back to my own childhood, all that time standing shamefully on my chair in maths lessons, and I tried to teach with humour and sensitivity, to make mental arithmetic fun rather than a blood sport.

In some schools where I worked 'supply' they were just grateful that you had kept all the children in the room and no chairs were thrown, as was the case in one school where the children all seemed to be at least 5 ft 10 and most had facial piercings and/or tattoos. The head teacher spent his days pacing up and down the corridors, looking like a battered old teddy bear, on the watch for signs of insurrection. It was all good experience. I also did a few full-time maternity covers which was great as I had missed forming day to day relationships with the same pupils, having some confidence that I was using their real names and of the camaraderie of being in work full time.

In key stage one where the children are still very needy, I was bombarded with good natured questions or comments from almost every parent each morning. This is standard if the school has a policy of allowing parents unfettered access to the class teacher every day and it is important for parents to keep the lines of communication open with staff. However, I soon realised that my memory was appalling, and I took to wearing a mini whiteboard around my neck so that I could jot down everything the parents mentioned, as the children filed in. Looking back a wad of post it notes might have been more discrete but would have been much easier to lose. These days I tend to forget that I've written myself a note and put it in my pocket, and at some point, I will inevitably have tried to blow my nose on it. The whiteboard system helped to an extent, but I would still look at the list later in the day and wonder how I had literally no idea what I had written hours earlier, I vaguely recognised my handwriting but beyond that most of it didn't ring any bells.

Things I must remember and act upon could include doctor/hospital appointments, wobbly teeth, poorly dog/hamster/grandparent, new dog/hamster/sibling, missing socks, hats, gloves, odd shoes, the wrong sized plimsoles, friendship issues, change of pick up time or who was collecting, dinner money, trip money, milk and fruit money, medical forms, medicine, allergy information, itchy things, earaches, nits, worries of multiple kinds (none which resulted in eyebrow plucking) questions about homework or schoolwork, equipment, uniform, non-uniform, birthday cake, diplomatic handing out of exclusive birthday party invitations etc etc. The vast majority of parents were supportive and grateful for the time and effort put in by staff to keep their children safe, happy and learning. However, it seemed as though there were a small number of parents who intentionally or not, made life more difficult.

One parent wanted staff to police the toilets and clean them down between uses (this was pre covid) in case her child came into contact with any chicken eggs. I should explain that it was Easter at the time, and the child had a suspected egg allergy, but had no official note from a doctor. In the end it was decided that this level of toilet attendance was impossible with our limited staff, so we bought a load of polystyrene eggs for the children to decorate instead, to minimise the chicken egg contamination risk. The twist to the story was that this child was friends with one of my own personal children and came to our house one night after school for tea. I was tired, and by this time had forgotten about the egg allergy (I didn't take my neck whiteboard home, foolishly) so after tea I made dozens of pancakes with all kinds of delicious toppings-the only thing I can reliably make for pudding. The child ate hungrily, asked for further helpings from my limitless supply and seemed to be thoroughly enjoying them, with no adverse reactions. The mum looked absolutely horrified when she came to pick the child up later and I don't think they came for tea again. I admit- I messed up, but at least the mystery over whether the egg allergy was a thing, in relation to pancakes anyway, was cleared up.

She got her own back in a wholesome mumsy sort

of way a few months later by offering a bag of wind-fall apples to my friend to make a pie with, while deliberately excluding me. My friend was offended because this suggested she looked as though she would be the type of mum who would make a nice pie with them, and I was offended because I obviously looked as though I was the type of mum who would be more likely to make cider.

When I worked in a different school I had a much more unreasonable complaint from an irate parent, one night after the Christmas disco. I was in my classroom looking at the aftermath and trying to summon up the energy to attempt to tidy some of the peripheral stuff away when I heard the shrill and unmistakable voice of one of my parents. (Just to clarify- not one of my biological parents, but one of the mums from my class) She was storming towards my room demanding to speak with me and I admit, I was a bit concerned- she was feisty and had a bit of a reputation for fighting. The reason for her fury was that I had allowed- in her mind perhaps even encouraged, her son to go home wearing somebody else's party clothes. I tried to appeal to her using logic- he had come to school in his uniform and brought his unnamed party clothes in an unnamed carrier bag. He had got himself changed at lunchtime and had seemed perfectly happy. Everyone else in his class had also changed into their party clothes and were happy too, and they'd had a brilliant time, sliding along the hall floor through stray peas and custard and screaming at the top of their lungs. The only problem that had arisen was the fact that he was apparently wearing someone else's stuff, maybe the brand was causing the offence, maybe it was from the wrong discount sports shop- perhaps it was even from 'Primani'.

My personal children always got supermarket clothes, because let's face it- they are beautiful when compared to the hand me down brown flared cords of my youth, and I could never understand the point of labels worn on the outside. Anyway, my defence, which she eventually (although reluctantly) accepted, was to calmly point out to her that if her child couldn't recognise his own party clothes, I am not sure how she expected me to. Am I supposed to have that knowledge too? To just 'know' what each member of my class wears when they are at home or at a party? That would just be weird.

Christmas was always a magical time in a primary school, and although I had stopped trying to push my dodgy playwriting on people, and we followed published playscripts, the stress of the school performance still played a part. There would always be one or two bum shufflers or nose pickers who would cause amusement in the audience. One boy managed to bum shuffle across the entire stage during the final song so that he could look at his mum and I remember the Head being cross about it afterwards. In my later teaching jobs I have often thought back fondly to that incident and compared it to the behaviour I was later to be confronted with. If only I had known at the time.

For a brief time, I ended up teaching my own personal children, which never helps the parent-child relationship. Once the bell went, the frantic working mum they had come into school with disappeared and was replaced by this cold-hearted, semi-professional woman who always gave them a hard time, never picked them for prizes and rarely gave them any credit publicly for their achievements. I was so anxious to avoid looking as though I was favouritising them that I probably went too far the other way. Once I even ignored my eldest having a hypo because I was worried about singling her out and giving her too much attention. Luckily one of my TAs was tuned in and sympathetically took action before it became an emergency, but I felt very guilty afterwards.

More guilt for the guilt box in my mind, which I am sure is an exclusively female or 'mum' thing. I read somewhere once that men are more easily able to compartmentalise their lives into boxes in their minds, an excellent, healthy and useful skill to have. One of these boxes is empty, there is nothing in there, and men (allegedly) have the ability to visit this box whenever they need to. This theory can be tested just by asking the men you know (or if you are a man, by asking yourself) what they are thinking about if they have a vacant, far off look in their eyes. If the answer is 'nothing' they could very well be telling the truth. If you identify as a gender other than male and have this empty gift box, enjoy and appreciate it.

Chapter 8 Snot, Pants and Performance Management

I taught one class in which a little girl had a permanent issue with snot. Her nostrils were sealed with translucent shiny green stoppers like the seals great African land snails form over the end of their shells during hibernation. It didn't appear to bother her at all, but it bothered me when I took the class swimming. She was splashing about and then popped up happily out of the water, face pink and radiant, nostrils flaring and clean. My smile froze as I knew with certainty that somewhere in the pool her green mucus plugs would be floating, waiting to be spotted, swallowed or stuck in somebody's hair.

Swimming always caused a bit of extra stress. It didn't seem to matter how many times the children were reminded to put their socks in their shoes and their pants somewhere sensible, we always had some item of clothing missing at the end of the session. Usually it was socks, but once it was an entire shirt. We were followed into the changing rooms by another school and suspected that things had got mixed up somehow in the lockers. This meant 30 children waiting for 20 minutes for another 30 children to come out of the pool, find all their belongings and then try to find the missing shirt amongst them. It was a nightmare, there were too many children, and too many carrier bags and wet towels. We were on a time challenge already with the bus booking, our schedule for the children's school lunches and our parent volunteers who needed to be back, and the shirt was inexplicably gone.. so the child had to go back to school naked underneath their school jumper, which wasn't good.

Teaching mainstream primary is fun, but hard work and your work life balance is in the hands of the leadership team and the head. I was having my 'performance management interview' with the Head teacher one afternoon and I knew he was likely to mention my planning files. Some schools demand a regular review of planning files, in addition to work scrutinies and lesson observations. I always had good lesson observations and the children made good progress, the evidence was in their books, but my planning was never followed exactly. I always went with what the children needed rather than what was planned and my paperwork was never organised, in fact the file often resembled a scrap book. To attempt to keep it somewhere near acceptable I would spend all day on a Sunday writing plans that were followed on a Monday but usually not recognisable by the Friday. Despite this, I was confident that he would be happy with my performance so I sat opposite him at his desk waiting for his analysis of the CASPA data generated from all the assessments of my class from the last couple of terms. This included detail about the core subjects English, Maths and Science and within those all the subsections; reading, writing, speaking and listening, shape, space, measure, number, living things, materials, forces etc. As well as the other 7 non-core or foundation subjects.

This Head teacher was excellent at detail. He loved statistics and knew the minutiae and percentages expected and attained by every child every term in all ten subjects and no doubt in swimming and uniform retention too. He completed his assessment of my assessments and asked me to photocopy the paperwork. I was glad to finally escape from the office, so I leapt up and went over to the copier. At the time all the staff wore walkie talkies because we had one child who suffered from epilepsy and if she had a seizure, it was important that her meds were administered quickly. The theory was that if we heard the bleeping of the walkie talkie we would communicate (calmly and sensibly) with whoever had set it off and the nearest staff member would run to the staffroom, get the meds and run to wherever the alarm had sounded. We were all terrified that the walkie talkies would set off their alarm-now I work in SEND and seizures are extremely commonplace and they are usually calmly dealt with in the classroom, with walkie talkies reserved for more unusual events. My walkie talkie was attached to the waistband of my trousers and as I leaned over the photocopier, I accidentally pressed the alarm button, which started to beep at an unbelievably loud volume.

The school was small and basically open plan, so to be honest, in an emergency we could have just shouted for help. I tried to unclip it from the band of my trousers but it was caught. The beeping continued, it was deafening. The head rushed from his room as I was trying to answer all the voices coming through my walkie talkie "Where are you?" "Do you need the meds?" "Who has set it off?" but my walkie talkie was still firmly attached to my trousers. I pulled and pulled and eventually it released from my trousers but was caught firmly on the lacy band of the pair of generous 'full briefs' I was wearing. I looked in horror as at least a foot of black elasticated pant material stretched out in front of me, stretching in the direction of the Head. Frantically, I continued to pull at the noisy machine and shouted into it "It's fine! It's me! It's a false alarm!", the top half of my body craned over the walkie talkie in desperation. The Head looked at me, looked at my pants, blushed rapidly and fled back to his room, muttering "Well it all looks to be in hand" just as the office filled with every spare staff member in the building. The size of my pants was legendary after that.

The level of accountability and scrutiny we face as teachers is continual and relentless. A friend of mine once said that if a plumber was coming to his house to fix a leak, he wouldn't expect him to produce an exact plan, with timings, to explain how he would achieve the outcome and observe him the whole time he was doing it. We would trust his professional judgement. Why are teachers not given the same freedom? Probably because teachers are generally disliked, maybe it's a genetic thing, which has altered the DNA of each generation in the same way that we have evolved to be wary of spiders or big cats. Most of us teachers are nice people these days, and we have to provide evidence to show that we have met over 40 professional standards during training and these are referred to in every lesson observation for ever and ever.

Care worn, sleep deprived and obsessed, we spend our time worrying about people we aren't related to, dream of assessment criteria, policy documents and where we are going to pick up a roll of silver foil and a spare pair of swimming trunks from before an 8:30 staff briefing. The 'to do list' is never, ever achieved and just gets longer and longer. The thing about teaching is that everybody has been to school and therefore has an opinion about what the job involves. The statistics for teachers leaving the profession and the rapid turnover of staff in most schools would suggest that it isn't as easy as many people think. Those people who belittle the difficulties of the job are, in my experience, the ones who are stressed out by their own children in school holidays and find the idea of entertaining half a dozen of them for a birthday party for a couple of hours exhausting. The recent difficulties thrust upon many families because of the corona virus has brought up lots of issues, and it seems as though many parents have a new found gratitude for the service that schools offer, even if their opinions of teachers haven't changed. Most of us love the classroom bit, but that is only half the story. Being accountable and responsible for measuring every single aspect of the achievement, development, safety and mental wellbeing of every student means that the paperwork and the mental stress is huge.

I look back on this period of time as the nappies decade, a blur of babywipes and sleepless nights. My personal life was becoming increasingly difficult, my husband hated his teaching job and things were not great between us. In an effort to change his career we decided to import 20 tonnes of mixed Indian granite and slate, via an old school friend who had relatives involved in the granite business in India. I know that sounds like an odd decision, but it seemed like a good gamble to take at the time, everyone loved granite worktops and the profits seemed worth the effort. A massive crane delivered it to my parents-in –law where it gradually sunk into the earth, but for a few years we made extra money working nights and weekends fitting kitchen worktops.

We extended the house, which was really a two up, two down cottage, and lived with my mum for 6 months while it was transformed into more of a family sized home. In 2004 and 2005 I gave birth to two beautiful sons and had a break from teaching for these two years. During this time, I helped with the granite shenanigans and ran the local toddler group. It gave me an outlet for my playdough habit, and I liked thinking of activities for the children, it was also an excuse to continue my little side addiction to collecting bits of rubbish and resources which could be turned into works of art. This is just a normal side effect of being a teacher, I don't need help for it or the interference from a TV show, and now I teach secondary, I've almost completely kicked the habit.

Chapter 9 Unpleasantness

After a major storm in 2008, the ground floor of our house was completely flooded, resulting in us having to live in rented accommodation for 6 months while it was fixed. This was not an easy time; things had not been easy for a while. The storm was continuing in our personal lives and it is confusing to know when you are in the middle of a storm whether it is ever going to end. This is the impossible thing about bad patches- nobody tells you how long a bad patch is meant to last before it is no longer a patch and becomes just bad.

From the outside, our lives were lovely. The village was like something from a storybook with a little stone church and a village green with trees to climb and conkers to collect. Chickens and children were safe to run free range through the village and because everybody knew everyone else, they were safe. We had village events, quiz nights and musical Burns nights in the village hall which were warmed by a huge open fire. We made the Christingles at our kitchen table for the village church at Christmas, leading on to raucous, spontaneous sledging during January and February and shared family Easter egg hunts at Easter. We watched the birth of spring lambs from the bedroom window and when the weather warmed up the children would run barefoot between the houses. Summers were punctuated by barbeques, beer, and games on the village green and the cycle would begin again. The village and its community were nothing short of magical.

My first husband and I were very young when we married, in our second year at university. The vicar who married us was friendly but shifty, he said he was too busy to attend the reception and it later became clear that he had made other plans. The following day he was in the 'Northern Echo' because he had run away with one of his married parishioners, causing a local scandal. My dad reckoned that's why he had insisted on cash for the service. After the reception (which boasted the cheapest buffet in the northeast and mainly comprised of mini sausage rolls), my wedding dress slowly fell apart. It was the excuse I needed to change back into my jeans and DMs for a BBQ outside, none of the random guests knew where the bride had gone, and Nelly the Elephant was inexplicably the first song to blast out from a friend's sound system.

Being in a serious relationship so quickly meant that university life was a bit different, but we did manage to do some fun student things. One weekend in February we hitch hiked to Paris- the truth was that a long-distance trucker had stopped at a service station in Lancashire to put his rubbish in the bin and we had climbed into his cab. He was too polite to explain the misunderstanding until we got to Dover.

Although I loved the little hamlet where we lived, loved the people there and the sense of community, the hills and green fields that surrounded us, my hens and vegetable patch, our cottage, its beams, the Aga and the open fires, and of course our four beautiful children, I was very unhappy in my relationship.

Gradually, year by year, my sense of self was eroded until I had no confidence left and no clear understanding of what was right and wrong. I was confused about what behaviour I should accept and what I should be justifiably uncomfortable or angry about. If I was offended or upset, it was because I was too sensitive. I was the boring wife, where was my sense of humour? if we went out, I was always the designated driver and responsible one who would take care of all the kids- our friends' kids and our own, which sometimes amounted to a dozen or so. I loved being with them, providing entertainment, toffee popcorn or pancakes, but this kindness was perhaps mistaken for martyrdom and people become complacent and disrespectful of martyrs. I would never have dared risk being drunk in case my eldest had needed me to calculate insulin or one of the children was poorly.

With things the way they were I needed to secure a permanent contract after doing fulltime temporary contracts and went for a job interview which happened to fall on World Book Day. I decided to go to the interview dressed as Jack AND his Beanstalk. I was dressed head to toe in green, in a costume crafted from stuff I'd found in a charity shop, my fabulous beanstalk draped around my neck and trailing on the floor behind me and for a more realistic effect I had added a few real runner beans. Despite developing a form of interview Tourette's and asking the students in my lesson observation if they wanted to 'smell my beans' they gave me the job. I was to start in the September, at a lovely village school teaching key stage one, to do key stage one SATS.

After that, the problems at home soon came to a head. I was photocopying at work when I suddenly started to cry and could not seem to stop. My friend asked what was wrong and when I told her some of the details of my marriage she simply said 'Well- it's out there now, you've said it, what are you going to do about it?'.

I decided that I had a choice, and I kept repeating this to myself, over and over again. This is such a powerful thought, even when the choice is having nothing, at least there is still a choice. Eventually, we parted that August, I left my home suddenly one day, with no belongings. I took the kids to my mum's house for the night, and we ended up staying for two years.

I tore them away from the place they'd been since they were born, a place we all had friends and roots, somewhere we all loved. I still find it difficult to think about the trauma this caused them, (you can imagine the state of the guilt box in my mind after this) but I still believe, despite the issues that they have all struggled with, that it would have been worse if I'd stayed. My family supported us with unbelievable generosity and kindness, my mum and stepdad helped to source clothes, beds, second-hand bikes and eventually converted their garage into a granny flat where they lived so that we could have 'the run of the house'.

It was hard, and for a long time I felt as if I was watching my life happen from behind a window. I had dulled emotions, as if I had been given anaes-thetic but was still able to move around. My future life plan had disappeared overnight, I suddenly had no partner to grow old with or plan holidays with. The good thing though, was that we all woke up in the morning in control of what kind of a day we would have and that was freedom, like being able to breathe clean air for the first time in years. It was undeniably a very difficult few months, no home of our own, no savings and a new job to start a month later, but practically speaking life was easier as a single mum. I could concentrate on looking after the children with no distractions, nobody making me feel guilty if I wanted to read them one more story at bedtime.

The next couple of years were hard, with court

dates and incidents to deal with. I didn't really confide in anyone so when I left, it was a surprise to a lot of people, especially when it became clear that there was no 'other' man involved. Things were eventually resolved but I left my relationship of almost two decades with nothing, there was apparently no money available to divide, no apparent assets either, but there's more to life than things and money.

A major part of my current role is to teach about relationships and am so much more educated now than I was. I understand how 'good' relationships can turn bad, how gradual the changes can be and what the warning signs are. I am passionate about raising awareness of what is and is not part of a healthy relationship. I now know that abuse can manifest in all areas of a person's life, emotional, mental, financial, sexual as well as physical, and I know that what unites them all is power and control. I feel that the experiences I have had have led me to the role I have now, and without that understanding I would not be effective or empathetic in that role.

That period of my life is still too painful to think about in any detail ten years later, and the ripples are still causing suffering. However, my ex is now apparently glorious to his current partner, and if that is true, I am honestly incredibly pleased for her.

Chapter 10 Holidays!

I carried on teaching as well as I could throughout this period and looking after my own children kept me going... In an effort to make it up to them for all the heartache they had suffered I did my best to give them as many good experiences as I could. The year after we left, I decided I would take them to Florida on my own, courtesy of my credit card. This was brave as they were all so little and it was brilliant -but also one of the most stressful holidays ever, and that's saying something when most of our family holidays ended up in A&E.

One particularly memorable year, we were lost in Paris for what felt like several months with a trailer tent and a map of Paris the size of a teabag. Our first and only ever visit to Euro Disney was a total disaster, it was the year that much of Cornwall was washed into the sea and Europe was blighted by torrential rain. Amongst other things, my ex-husband became enraged by the poor quality of a Disney rattle we had bought for our elder son and ended up throwing it across the shop at the cashier, who was denying we'd bought it from there (despite it having Disney written all over it). He stormed off with a pushchair and nearly barged right over the top of a poor man who was being given CPR after collapsing on the ground outside the Magic Kingdom castle.

On another holiday with the girls when they were tiny, we mistook a rash on the older child's tummy for meningitis (it turned out she had given herself the rash by rubbing against the metal edge of the caravan table). She was given a shot of penicillin and blue lighted to hospital for the night, which was fun. These were not unusual events, there were so many that they blur into each other and merely form another hazy memory in the nappies decade.

I managed to save hundreds of pounds on my Florida flights, with a little help from some good friends. The snag was that there was a 6 hour 'lay-over' in Atlanta and the flight times were awful. We stayed in the cheapest Disney hotel possible and were all squashed into one room, with fold down beds in a wooden chalet type thing located about a mile from the main building.

It was good, the Florida sun was shining, and all was going well until my eldest child's insulin pump broke. This meant a return to calculating insulin doses and multiple injections and a lot of time on the phone trying to get a replacement sent out. The pump was American so I stupidly thought we could get another sent directly- but apparently it would have had to go through English customs, which still makes no sense to me. To add to the fun, we had been swimming in a waterpark when a big tidal wave had scooped her up and dropped her, injuring the skin on the top of her foot, and it had started to fester. I decided it probably needed some medical attention, so I rang the Disney medical help phone number provided in the room information. It was like some sort of horrible joke. I was greeted by a ridiculous Disney employee asking if I was having a nice day and when I told her of my worries, she faked sympathy noises and told me what I needed was an ambulance. While I was on the phone to this imbecile there seemed to be a kerfuffle happening outside and all the children started shrieking 'FIRE'. I thanked her, told her I just wanted some antibiotic cream or something, not an ambulance, and that I'd have to go as there appeared to be a fire outside my room. She skipped straight back into her Disney script and sang;

'OK! have a nice day!'

'But I won't, will I?' I replied curtly.

Outside our wooden chalet room there was a matching wooden decking area which was indeed on fire. It seemed to be quickly gaining strength and spreading before our eyes. I felt as if I was on a reality TV game show and viewers were paying extra to add more challenges just for the fun of it to watch me squirm. I have felt like this several times over the years, like a contestant on an even nastier version of The Truman Show. We were far from the main building and the lovely Florida climate meant that the flames were spreading nicely- there was no time to go for help. Using the useless and totally impractical miniature cups supplied in our tiny bathroom we formed a tag team refilling them from the equally pointless little sink and amazingly we eventually managed to extinguish it. Triumphant, but now scoring 10/10 on the stress scale I took a deep breath. This was hard on my own. I knew something needed to be done about the festering foot but that she would probably survive the night. Weighing up the options I decided we needed a waffle- Mickey's head had to be on a plate and I badly needed a glass of wine.

On the way to the main building my other daughter stood on a spike which pierced both her flip flop and her foot, and I wasn't even surprised. We stumbled and limped on towards the waffles, leaving a trail of blood behind us, and after the wine the whole situation seemed so much better. It is only recently that my children have admitted that they had started the fire using a piece of glass, a hobby of theirs that I had completely forgotten about. My daughter said 'Don't you remember mum? The boys were always trying to set fire to things with magnifying glasses?'

The following day we had planned to use our free tickets to Legoland. The boys were massive Lego fans, so it was bound to be a success. We climbed on to the coach and settled down for a fairly long journey, I don't know if it was a long journey but that's how I remember it, trundling on and on for hours and hours. As we eventually pulled in to the vast and fairly empty carpark, there was an announcement- the coach would be back to pick us up 10 hours later. My heart sank. We all liked Lego, but surely 10 hours was excessive? With trepidation, we studied the map and slowly walked around all the available attractions- little lego cities, the wonders of the world made out of lego, famous legoey landmarks, more little lego cities.. and then we wondered how to spend the next 8 hours. We slowly looked at the menu options in the canteen, ordered pizza and then made a game out of eating it as slowly as possible… half an hour gone. By then it was probably approaching 11am..Then, in the distance and to our excitement and delight we spotted a first aid station, and I still remember the feeling of triumph and relief. At last, an attraction I was interested in. We trooped in, greeted the man over-enthusiastically, and revealed our gifts to him. The man brightened up immediately, he had obviously been waiting for this kind of excitement for a very long time. He took a good look at my elder daughter's festering foot and my younger daughter's foot piercing and happily supplied us with antibiotic cream, dressed both their feet very professionally and sent us on our way to enjoy the remaining 7 hours. Surviving Florida on my own with four young children felt like an accomplishment, if I could do that then I was not afraid to do anything.

We went all over the place, every weekend was busy and I tried to give them as many happy memories as possible, despite the chaos that usually gravitated in our direction. Sometimes we would get lost, sometimes I would accidentally book a truly horrible room in a red-light district somewhere, occasionally it would all end in tears. Always, however, I would pull myself together again and we would carry on. My younger daughter once responded to my enthusiastic "Come on, we are going on an adventure!" by begging with me; "Please mum, can we not just go where we've planned?"

Chapter 11 Adrenalin

Eventually things got a little easier, we were surviving. I felt as though I was coming back to life, I was beginning to have my own opinions again and whenever I got the opportunity I would walk for miles, often conquering mountains in the beautiful Lake District, which was only an hour away. I think I have probably put my children off walking as we did it so often, in all kinds of weather and sometimes mistakenly with the promise of a drink and a snack in a pub which did not exist anymore or was shut.. I started going to spinning classes and made friends with new people who gave me goals to aim for. I decided to raise money for a children's brain tumour charity Abbie's Army by attempting to climb the highest 3 mountain peaks nationally, within 24 hours. Thanks to the kindness of friends and family, and a few fundraising events, we donated over two thousand pounds in the end. The three peaks attempt was scheduled for June. My mother was as usual, supportive but also seemed irritated and when I got to the bottom of it, she genuinely believed I would probably die and leave her with all my children to look after. There were a group of us doing the challenge, my good friend Lydia and I were joined by others from around the country who were all raising money for different charities. The minibus journey to Scotland was tedious and took hours, and many of us felt wobbly and travel sick by the time we got there. However, Ben Nevis was beautiful and it was good to stretch our legs at last. The air was fresh and after an hour or two of walking I had worked up a thirst. Our mountain guide stopped to admire one of the crystal-clear streams running down next to the path. I knew the rules-never drink from a mountain stream- but the evil guide said he had never known anyone to become ill after drinking this pure and delicious water. Stupidly I decided to give it a go and so I filled my flask with it. We made it to the top and through the June snow, had a quick look at the incredible view and then walked back down the mountain and back on the minibus. We were then to travel to Scarfell Pike, which we were to climb that night.

This was going to be another long journey from Scotland to the Lake District. Unfortunately, the Ben Nevis water in my insides was turning into molten lava and becoming quite a personality in its own right, churning and boiling. I reached the top of Scafell with my walking buddies and then had my first taste of fell running as I scampered back down most of the mountain in search of a toilet. They must have thought I was showing off or that they had offended me in some way. I have no photos from the top of Scarfell from the three peaks and how I managed to survive the turmoil unsullied still amazes me. Luckily I hung on until we reached a service station on the way to Wales where I ate an entire packet of imodium. Snowden was last on the list and thankfully I managed it without incident.

Now that I understand more about mental health and resilience I can see that I was doing the things that people are advised to do if they are suffering from depression. Mine was reactive depression, I was reacting to a situation, so I did not take any medication although I had some very dark times. The advice is to exercise, try new things, join new groups, spend time with positive people, get fresh air, give to others, look around you and notice the beauty in the world, have goals- all these things I did without understanding that I needed to do them in order to heal. In every dark moment there was also something to laugh about and finding the humour in the bleakest of situations was vital in getting through it. My family were there to help, and it also soon became apparent who my real friends were, which was in some cases surprising and in others, disappointing.

I continued with my teaching responsibilities and parenting the best I could, and eventually we moved out of mums and into rented accommodation until I could buy a house. It wasn't as nice as the cottage the children had been taken home to after they were born, I wasn't allowed chickens and it felt new and characterless, but it was ours as long as I could keep up with the horrendous mortgage payments. Money was so tight at this time that I would even keep potato peelings, fry them and offer them up as homemade crisps. The house was in a small village and positioned at the entrance to a large estate, exactly the kind of place where everyone twitches their curtains to check if the neighbour is cutting the grass or washing their car yet.

As a single mother with four children, I was excellent entertainment for them, the old couple opposite even admitted 'tuning in' at 8 every morning to watch me attempting to get them all in the car with the right bags and the right uniforms on. The brief clarinet phase added extra pressure, and so did swimming lessons or PE, so when my students forget their things or say they have left them at their dad's/mum's house I am always sympathetic. I saw this smug old couple standing together at their upstairs window, watching us one morning when I was running late. I'd bundled a half-naked boy into the back, thrown his clothes in after him, and hoped that he had most of it on by the time we got to school. They commented to me afterwards about it as though that had been their favourite episode so far. The chaos of school mornings continued into secondary school. One morning I received a call at work from one of my sons to say that they had each got one of their shoes wrong, as both boys had similar black school shoes. One son was at primary, the other at secondary, in two different places. The younger was therefore wearing one of his own shoes and a massive shoe, the older was wearing one of his own and a tiny shoe. I had to embroil confused grandparents to travel around the county playing shoe swapping until they both had a matching pair. On another occasion I watched with horror as one of them ran happily into the playground with a pair of pants wafting from the hood of his jacket where they had spitefully velcroed themselves. The embarrassment seemed to be made worse because I was a local teacher- people love it if you mess up. These days I am happy to dispel the myths that we are any more organised or competent as parents, and I couldn't care less if people who don't know me pass judgement.

Things were ticking along quite peacefully until one night, very randomly, I had a dream that I was working in a SEND school near the coast. The next day I thought it might be a good idea to check out if there were any jobs and to my surprise, there was a job which weirdly matched the one from my dream. I am not superstitious, but my grandparents were both heavily involved in the Spiritualist church (I didn't mention this at the Convent interview) and they would always be looking for 'signs', so there's maybe a bit of something that way inclined in my DNA. My mum, despite being a regular church goer, will still excitedly suggest a Ouija board in times of uncertainty. I have only ever done one with her once, when I was young. The apparent outcome was that my first husband would end up working for 'berol' which I believe is a pen manufacturer, although there was some disagreement over whether it was 'bero', the flour people. My grandad was a baker, so that was a much more acceptable interpretation. So far as I know, this prediction has not come true so far.. The irony of this strong belief in spiritualism is that my grandad chose not to contact my poor grandma after his death, which I know she found infuriating. Every time we met up I would ask gently 'Have you heard anything from grandad yet?' and the answer was always 'No, nothing yet'. In their last home together, a tiny bungalow, they had a little wooden cabinet with fancy metal handles and its drawers were full of their best silver cutlery. It stood next to my grandad's armchair in the living room, and the people from the spirit world would apparently use this to channel their messages. After grandad died, the cutlery was 'spookily' silent, and after my grandma's death, my uncle was so freaked out at the idea that the cutlery would start up again that he put duct tape across all the drawers, before storing them securely in his attic.

According to the advert, a secondary SEND school over on the northeast coast needed a 'Literacy and Communication coordinator' for the primary department, which was a management role. The small amount of extra money would be welcome, and I felt like I was ready to change direction, regain control over my life and step out of my comfort zone after 17 years of Primary teaching. When I first qualified, I didn't want to be anything more than a good classroom teacher, so I had no interest in applying for promotions. I felt it was inappropriate to climb the career ladder without being confident and proficient in the role of teacher- I have since observed that not everyone has this mindset. For some people teaching is like any other job and the aim is to climb as high as possible and earn as much as possible. Managers sometimes lack teaching experience, and, in some cases, the life experience and compassion needed to make the right decisions, but I expect this is the same in many organisations.

I decided to investigate the job a little further. Asking around, nobody I knew really understood the job title, and when I researched the school, it seemed that it was in a lot of trouble. It was in a very deprived part of the county and OFSTED had put it into 'Special Measures' which means that it had been judged, rightly or wrongly, to be a disaster in a lot of areas.

My family thought I was foolish to apply, but I had a good feeling about it. I had spent the last few years fuelled by adrenalin, fighting my way back into being an independent person who could now make their own choices. I knew it would be totally different from the career I'd had so far- my experience of teaching secondary aged students was limited to covering lessons at The Convent and my special needs experience was also limited to a few children with moderate learning difficulties such as dyslexia or ADHD and one pupil with Down's Syndrome. However, I was passionate about teaching English, and I knew that the job would not appeal to many people, with the situation the school was in, so with nothing to lose (except what remained of my sanity), I applied.

Chapter 12 Finding my Mojo

I was invited to an interview, which was daunting and involved presenting a powerpoint about how I would single handedly improve everything about the school. I did not mention a golden lasso or being able to spin around quickly, but I do remember the last slide finished with the snowman Olaf from Frozen waving goodbye, which I suppose is comparable in weirdness to the 'smell my beans' interview. I wasn't expected to do a teaching demonstration for this job, which was unusual and looking back I can now completely understand why that might have been.

I liked the school; it was modern and spacious. The area beyond the security doors and the reception was very civilised, clean and stylish. The furniture was square and low, and the colours contrasted with vibrant blocks of colour on the walls. I waited nervously and was ushered eventually into a conference room where I have little idea of what I said. I noticed that the area which contained the students was behind this sanitized and stylish management area. It could be seen through a toughened glass wall but only accessed through another security point.

The management who had interviewed me were saying their goodbyes and I was about to leave when I considered that it might be a good idea if I could have a look around the actual school. Nervous glances were exchanged, and I had to wait again while they thought about it. Eventually another member of staff appeared, the charming Mr P, and offered to show me around. I liked it- it was a school which catered for pupils from 4-19 years and the job I had applied for was in the secondary department but overseeing English and communication in the primary school. I had been told that there would be the opportunity to move around and teach different age groups if I wanted to. Mr P and the other staff I met were all friendly and welcoming and many of the students I was introduced to obviously had a range of additional needs but seemed happy. There was a hydro pool and sensory room with soft furniture and lights which changed colour if they were touched and tubes of water which bubbled gently as air was fed through them. Some classrooms were similar to mainstream classrooms, but I noticed there were fewer student places. Corridors were wide enough to accommodate wheelchairs and some classrooms had a track on the ceiling with an electrical hoist attached, operated by a control pad to enable staff to help students in and out of wheelchairs.

The primary classrooms were noisy, and some had few resources and displays, but it was explained that for some children it is not helpful to have too many things available or too much to stimulate their senses. I later understood that it was also partly because some of these children will 'go into crisis' and destroy things, so it was practically unsafe or difficult to maintain role play areas or allow free access to resources.

A few days later I received a phone call to say I'd got the job and to check if I was happy to work in the secondary part of the school. I was excited as I knew this was going to be completely different from the teaching I had done before.

From the first day I felt as though I had been dropped in the deep end, in a pool full of treacle, on a completely different planet. On my first morning I arrived early but was unsure where to park, I could see a staff car park behind a barrier, but it was impossible to get into it without a key card. In the end I abandoned my car in a dodgy looking back street, which wasn't great as I had armloads of stuff to carry in and the locks on my car doors didn't work, however I was pleasantly surprised to find that my car was still there at the end of the day.

The school was relatively new, built in a small pit village that had never recovered from the closing of its colliery in the 1980s. It was built amongst rows of red brick terraces, many boarded up with shuttered windows. Shops on the main street were few and far between and the area felt somehow disappointed with itself and a little bit drunk and angry. From the upstairs windows of the school the unfriendly and grey North Sea could be seen, and later, when I got chance to explore the shoreline, it didn't seem much more attractive. The beach was darkened with sea coal and littered with rubbish and dog dirt, which I imagine made the weekend job of collecting sea coal even trickier for some of our students.

The first tutor group I was assigned to were a group of students with 'SLD' (severe learning difficulties) with one PMLD student (with profound and multiple learning difficulties) and teaching them was totally different to anything I had done in my previous lives teaching. There were about 6 students in the class with a support assistant (or two on a good day), their abilities were more in line with nursery or key stage one levels of development, but they were teenagers, with teenage interests and hormones. Some had proudly retained their childhood interests and still enjoyed a bit of Peppa Pig or Mr Tumble.

Often students with additional needs have sensory issues which need to be understood- they might respond positively to different multisensory activities or they may be repulsed or upset by certain things. At first it felt impossible to know what everybody needed, it was non-stop and at times felt as though we were fire-fighting, responding to incidents or needs rather than steering the course of events with any sort of plan. There were times when things were calm and the class were focussed on the same topic, but this was the exception rather than the norm. All the training and experience I had previously drawn on in my teaching jobs was mostly irrelevant, but having children of my own may have helped me to empathise. Those snappy quick paced lesson starters were faintly ridiculous here and very easily ignored, people could suddenly just wander off and it was hard to hold everybody's interest and very difficult to record any work, let alone show progress.

Some of the students were big people- much taller than me, which is unusual anyway and something I found strange after teaching small people for so long, perhaps it was something to do with the sea air. Every class was a mixture of characters and I soon found that their needs were diverse, unpredictable and fascinating. Their back stories were amazing, awe inspiring and occasionally horrifying. Some of the students had no issues at birth and had started out just like any 'mainstream' or neurotypical and physically healthy child, but had then developed illnesses or life changing conditions which had led them to need specialist provision.

There were children who were suffering from un-believably cruel medical conditions which I never knew existed, such as Duchenne muscular dystro-phy and Batten's disease. These conditions mean that the child's health and faculties deteriorate over time until they lose the ability to walk and func-tion and their lives are ultimately, prematurely cut short. It is a privilege to work with children who have a limit on their time, they still have a right to an education and many love school. Their par-ents or carers often need a sense of normality and some respite from the relentlessness of caring and worrying. Soon after I started this job however, a student in sixth form died and it struck me that this was going to be harder than I'd anticipated.

The uniqueness and range of students who at-tended the school was staggering and the levels of help they needed were as individual as they were. Some needed physical help to move or eat and some needed help with personal care. Some were more physically able but severely disadvantaged when it came to learning.

Other students were fine physically but had hidden disabilities like Autism or ADHD, which often came with behavioural difficulties. Some had amazing talents, could sing or dance beautifully or were cre-ative artistically, some exceptionally good at maths or English. I had never been in such an interesting workplace, and I loved it.. The staff there were, despite the damning OFSTED reports, highly skilled and generally very lovely people. It was fascinating to watch them address the needs of the students and I tried to learn as much as I could. Although I was in a middle management role, it reminded me very much of working at McDonalds- I worked there briefly in the summer after my degree and was immediately given a badge with 'MANAGER' written on it. This meant that I wore a white shirt when I cleaned the toilets, and I was given the additional perk of scraping the gum off the undersides of the tables. At this school I had a high viz jacket rather than a badge and had to stand guard during the chaos at the start and end of the day, often breaking up fights.

What became apparent was the importance of working with staff who really knew the young people individually. Each student had an extensive EHC (Education and healthcare) plan but there is no better way of getting to understand how to work with somebody than to talk with and watch other experienced staff interacting with them.

The key to it all was relationships, and I firmly believe this is the key to all the good things in life and to all the lessons we need to learn. I was lucky to have a classroom next to some excellent teachers, I'll call them Mrs W and Miss S and they helped me in so many different ways. I still work with one of these ladies but in a different school and the other has left the profession and is now a successful artist and maker of fabulous learning resources for small people. I watched what they did and it became clear that each student needed a different approach which relied on maintaining a positive relationship with staff. They practiced the concept of 'unconditional positive regard' which meant that poor behaviour choices were acknowledged, discussed and forgiven, and a fresh start was immediately granted.

This is different from what I had seen happen sometimes in mainstream, when a child slowly messed up throughout the day and went from having their name or photo on the happy green spot on the traffic light display, down to shameful amber and inevitably to criminal red. Often there was no fresh start until the next day, and little motivation for them to fix things. In a special school setting minor behavioural issues are often overlooked and ignored and staff carefully choose their battles. Even when a poor behavioural choice had been picked up by teacher, the students always had the chance to redeem themselves and were always given the opportunity to succeed. The ethos was tirelessly positive, creative, imaginative and nurturing. My new colleagues taught me to make sensory resources, including mats made from laminating pouches, filled with water and glitter or anything interesting, and sealed with a set of hair straighteners. They advised me on how to tackle literacy and numeracy, making my tasks exciting, engaging and practical. I was introduced to the joy of mark making in shaving foam and so many other ideas, if I was stuck or stressed, they were there to help.

One student in my new tutor group had 'oppositional defiance disorder' which was tricky. He was blonde and wiry, and almost completely non-verbal, with the exception of the odd really offensive swear word which he dropped like a bomb at the most unexpected times. It turned out that the most successful technique to use was to ask him to do the opposite of what you wanted. He had a tendency to flee the classroom whenever he got the chance and would stand glaring at people from amongst the coats and bags where they hung on a wall in the corridor. One of us would have to casually pretend to notice him in passing and comment how pleased we were that he was exactly where we wanted him to be. He would look a little annoyed and conflicted for a few moments and then put his head down and suddenly dart back inside the classroom. He could not deal with praise, it was confusing and distressing for him. This turned everything that I had learned so far in my teaching career upside down, it is a natural instinct to give praise and rewards, so praising him for the wrong things took a bit of getting used to. Once he was back in the classroom he would stand at the back and continue to glare quietly at his classmates and staff, but when praised again for not sitting down, he would sit down.

Meanwhile another member of the class may have discovered that throwing multilink cubes at somebody was far more entertaining than counting them, much to the distress of the others, and somebody else may have been quietly eating something inedible. This could be happening just as the beeping started to warn staff that the mechanical tube feed machine had finished for the student who needed a 'peg feed' directly to the stomach, or any number of other incidents could be happening all at once.

Another interesting student had an unusual type of autism called 'PDA' and combined with ADHD it made things very challenging for everyone. He was a unique and very likeable character, with a fantastic sense of humour, but his anxiety meant that he could respond very unexpectedly when he felt threatened. This could happen in times of transition, moving from one activity to another or from one place to another. Even stopping to eat lunch or transitioning back inside after break time could set him off. He had a tendency to take off his clothes and spin round, so it was important to allow him to do this somewhere private and to try to help him to regulate his behaviour so that this didn't continue into adulthood, as that would obviously cause him some problems. We succeeded eventually and over time he settled- so long as he was pursuing his specialist interests, he was usually happy. He particularly enjoyed historical disasters and I have taught a number of students with ASC who have enjoyed learning about the Titanic. These students can become experts, the autism sometimes giving them the ability to concentrate, research and remember details in a way that neurotypical people find really challenging.

Once a week we would take them swimming to the local leisure centre, and this seemed to take all morning. Every student needed help with changing clothes and most needed help with intimate care so it was a physically tiring job, and it was stressful trying to keep them together and safe, although having fewer students meant that we were in theory less likely to lose articles of clothing. There was also always the chance of accidental bad language leaking out into the general public, either from students or staff, but we usually managed without too many problems. It was upsetting when we saw people staring at our little group or whispering unkind comments to each other. To us they were completely normal, they were just being themselves and over time it felt as though the rest of the world were the odd ones. I soon found 'mainstream' children strangely precocious. After initially being zapped so far out of my comfort zone I felt as if I had landed in the twilight zone, I was starting to relax and enjoy the new challenge. I also began to think about how to help to sort out some of the issues the school had been having as a whole and met with colleagues to set about organising different baseline assessments in English, so that we all knew where we were. I loved it, loved meeting new people and trying to understand the needs of the young people I was working with and loved the challenge of trying to make things better.

Chapter 13 Challenges!

After a couple of terms and my trial by fire in the SLD class I was moved into a class to teach students with MLD (young people with moderate learning difficulties) and I started teaching English across the school. The other staff who taught English were excellent and very supportive, one was so proficient in using sign language that she used it constantly, even on nights out, which was amazing to watch but must have been exhausting. The students who were broadly identified as MLD were generally lively, disruptive, streetwise, cheeky and very likeable. Some were extremely challenging and a few were violent. The level of violence from a small minority surprised me but my history of being with somebody unpredictable served me well and I was pretty much bomb proof, showing no outward signs of stress. That doesn't mean I would be pushing myself to the front of the queue if an incident occurred, but I didn't flinch if something was happening.

I remember once when a very bright boy with ASC (autistic spectrum condition) had got hold of an eight-foot-long wooden pole with a metal hook on the end of it which was used to open high windows. He was 'in crisis' and spinning this pole around himself like a furious jazz band baton twirler, smashing it off walls and furniture and aggressively threatening staff or students who were unlucky enough to be in his way as he moved through the school. Nobody could have got near enough to him to physically restrain him without suffering a serious injury, but eventually his form tutor managed to talk him into putting the pole down- another example of the magic of positive relationships. Later on he went back into 'crisis' and his form tutor was called again to try to take a pair of scissors from him. He had somehow weaponed himself up and taken control of that room I'd had my interview in, camped out under the large table like a malevolent hermit crab.

Others were violent towards themselves, whatever they'd suffered was expressed by very disturbing behaviour, including one afternoon when it was found that a girl had written messages all over the toilet walls in her own blood. Trying to get mental health support for young people is not easy and the local CAMH service is still overstretched. You'd have to display some extremely disturbing behaviour before you were taken seriously, and I might remember it wrongly, but I have a feeling that the blood on the toilet walls didn't even summon much help. Recently this problem has been recognised and there has been more funding put in place which will hopefully improve things. In my experience though, special schools generally fall off the radar, even though statistically there is now abundant proof that the number of students with additional needs who suffer from mental health problems is much higher than it is in mainstream schools.

The MLD students often presented different issues and needs from the SLD students, they were often worldly wise and had particular sets of skills (I think that is a quote from a film, but I can't remember which one). The school had a high staff turnover, due to the recent unpleasantness, and so they had a few tricks up their sleeves for new staff. I realised that this was probably why doing a lesson observation at the interview could have been the stuff of nightmares, and why they had cleverly avoided introducing me to these students on my first visit.

Many students had been adversely affected by childhood trauma. The impact of adverse childhood experiences (ACEs) is now becoming more recognised as studies in the US have proved repeatedly that there is a link between toxic stress and later physical and mental health problems. The number of adverse experiences has a direct correlation to the likelihood of a range of problems, including negative life choices and later illness. It was personally very challenging to learn about the impact of ACEs as I counted up how many my personal children would be saddled with and wondered what the impact of their childhood trauma would be. This knowledge added to the everyday 'mother guilt' in the guilt box that comes with the job of motherhood and I still reflect on whether anything could have been done differently for my own children. The result of ACES can include learning difficulties, and over the last few years teaching students with additional needs, and getting to know their histories, it became very obvious to me that many of them had suffered more in their short lives than many adults. The research I read about explained why they displayed the behaviours or difficulties they did.

Other students had suffered direct or indirect physical abuse which had in extreme circumstances, damaged them irreparably. One child had been held by the legs and swung around by a caregiver and had received a life changing head injury. Another suffered from foetal alcohol syndrome- the child was left with serious behavioural and learning difficulties and was likely to suddenly attack staff and other students. She would be happily scribbling away one minute and then fly at someone and bite them hard enough to draw blood, with no provocation or warning. Some students had missed so much school through illness or lifestyle choices of parents that they needed extra support. Some had suffered from cancer and been left with blindness, learning difficulties or other physical problems.

We had a few traveller children who came from families who did not read or write much themselves and because they survived and functioned in society without much formal education they did not really see the point of school. Communicating with these parents was therefore often difficult as they could not understand letters and often did not answer their phones. I went with a colleague to visit a traveller family one day, to discuss the persistent absence of their son, as the relationship between home and school seemed to be breaking down.

I was apprehensive as I knew it could have been a tricky meeting but when we got to the house the boy's dad was welcoming. We went into the small front room, which was busy with traveller artefacts, ceramic horses, paintings and models of travelling wagons etc and had a cup of tea with him. He needed to explain his point of view to us- his culture was his life, his priority and he wanted his son to be proud of it. He was having to live in a house but didn't enjoy it and was therefore anxious that his son was properly educated in traveller culture-against that context, school was unimportant. I understood, but still found it frustrating because from what I had seen of his son, he would have probably been fine in mainstream school if he had attended more in primary. He was quick to pick up information and skills and had the potential to do well academically. Like some other traveller parents, they obviously loved their children but would not support them with schoolwork, and they were legally protected if they chose to take their child out of school for long periods to travel, as that was their culture.

When the Appleby fair was on, we had high numbers of student absences the week before the fair and the week afterwards. Some students would physically defend their heritage and pick fights with other 'wannabe gypsies' who lacked the proper family tree. Some went to trade horses and some just went for the social side. I have since worked with several traveller students, many of whom do not need to worry about academic success or needing to gain qualifications to get a job as their families are extremely wealthy. One of these used the loophole of being allowed to travel during term time to indulge in lengthy holidays to Florida each year. A small number of students including travellers, wannabe travellers and non-travellers were involved in local crime and were well known to the local police.

Despite the ever changing challenges and the one hour commute each way I perversely looked forward to work and had found my mojo again. All the time we were in special measures we had constant visits from inspectors, OFSTED, HMI, advisors or members of management from other schools, or just randoms who appeared with no explanation. There was usually an unfamiliar face in my classroom and I would have no idea whether they were a volunteer, a supply LSA or an inspector and in the end it didn't bother me.

Being in special measures was a bit like when you are in the middle of childbirth - you know it will end eventually but until that time you accept the pain and let go of your inhibitions, resigned to having to display your vulnerable bits to strangers. Luckily, the feedback was always positive so I carried on pretending that I knew how to handle these challenging youths.

Chapter 14 I don't get paid enough for this...

Meanwhile, the new faces from the supply agency would come and go- there was now only one agency who were willing to send teachers over the top to our particular front line, the young people were honing their battle skills. One morning I heard an eruption of laughter and a loud kerfuffle from across the corridor, I was in one of only a few first floor classrooms which had a shared central landing area with a glass mezzanine which looked down into the dining hall space below. I had a free lesson, so I went to the door ready to help if I was needed and was just in time to see the latest in a long line of supply teachers storm out of the 'tech suite' opposite. He was dressed smartly in a suit, obviously he had been hoping for the best that morning, but his face was red as he angrily strode past me, heading for the stairs.

"I don't get paid enough for this s**t!", he raged loudly enough for the whole upper floor to hear, which is probably the kind of outburst that could get you sacked, had he not been walking out anyway. The boys (they were mainly boys and that's not unusual) were jubilant at hearing that, and a massive cheer went up. "Eleven seconds!" they shouted. It turned out they had been timing how long he would stay in the classroom and that was apparently a new record for them. It's always nice to have a target to aim for at school. They gave all new teachers a rough ride at first, but I remember the day when I realised I was probably accepted by them, or most of them anyway. I had been about to receive a load of verbal abuse at close range from one of the scarier year 11 boys when another student, who was respected by his peers and equally fierce, told him to back off. "She's alright" he said, "leave her" and it was worth more than any mention in an OFSTED report. I think they thought I was 'alright' because I was genuinely interested in their stories, and I kept turning up. I also had a stash of custard creams in the cupboard and sometimes our English lessons would turn into 'speaking and listening' sessions which involved them just chatting about what was going on in their lives while having a mug of coffee or tea (no saucers here) always with at least two sugars.

I usually spent lunchtimes in my classroom and one day I was unexpectedly caught up in a hostage/barricade situation. I looked up from my faffing to see a very angry looking young man from one of my year 11 groups quietly enter my room. He did not speak, and I could see he was white with rage. This young man had a history of violence in school, he liked to protect the honour of his lady and also liked to defend his right to not follow instructions, so it could have been a very tricky situation indeed. I thought it best to keep my distance and pretended not to watch while he calmly picked up every desk and chair in the classroom and piled them up against the door that led to the landing, there was no other door through which to escape. The pile of furniture was eventually above our heads, a great heap of metal, he had done a good job. Nobody would have been able to see in through the slit of a window in the door, even if there had been somebody around. When he finished and there was no furniture except the heavy teacher's desk left to move, he seemed a bit calmer and eventually sat down on the floor, sweating. I got him a cup of tea, two sugars, and a couple of custard creams and sat near him (although not too close) and asked if there was something wrong. He told me all about his affairs of the heart, his woman, who was in year 10, had ended it with him because he'd been 'talking' to another girl (talking doesn't mean talking these days). After a while he was calm again and together we quietly dismantled the barricade, and he went off to his next lesson. Nobody noticed. I mentioned it later to some colleagues and they barely lifted an eyebrow.

There were phones in the classrooms, on which we could apparently call for back up, but nobody in the hermetically sealed stylish office/management area ever responded to them and students tended to phone 999 whenever they got the opportunity. The police car was almost a daily sight below my classroom window, which was very distracting. One student famously called the emergency services because they believed the maths lesson they were in was boring.

I taught one young man who was particularly well known to the local police for his arson attempts. We were sharing news from the weekend one Monday morning when this young man launched into his tales from the dark side, or the bright side, depending on whether the fires were lit or not. These were very different disclosures from the news we would share in my days as a primary teacher, when the sea of innocent little faces would be bursting to tell about a new puppy or a chocolate cake, or the discovery of a particularly splendid pinecone. Adam, a tall, gangly youth with a big grin (I just made up that name to protect his identity) declared resolutely this Monday morning that he was turning his back on his life of crime. This was a shock, to me and his classmates, and I was intrigued to know what had turned him around. He was a natural storyteller and so he explained. The police had turned up again at his door and wanted to question him about a local fire. They asked whether he was responsible, as he had so many previous fire related convictions. He said that he had stood there for a while, on his doorstep, thinking about it and eventually he had told them that they would have to be more specific- he couldn't remember how many fires he had lit off the top of his head or where they were- he needed more information. He was arrested for it and taken to the station where his clothes and belongings were taken away and he was given a paper onesie to wear. The humiliation of the onesie had been enough to deter him from committing any further crimes. He was a young man who liked his designer clothes, original or knock-off, and he wasn't going to be seen dead in a paper onesie again. Or so he said on that Monday, although I still look out for him in every episode of 'Canny Cops' or 'Police Interceptors' and I haven't spotted him so far, which is good.

The police would also attend sometimes when the students would abscond over the bizarrely low perimeter walls. Our responses to these incidents changed all the time, sometimes we were told to ignore them, sometimes we were told to try to stop them, sometimes we would follow on foot or by car and occasionally the police were called. At break-times all staff were expected on the yard as soon as the bell went, which was impossible if you taught on the first floor, and by the time we had got to the yard something bad would inevitably have happened. Apart from the attractions of the perimeter fence, there were other delights for the students to enjoy, which included a random rusty old container which had been inexplicably dumped on the yard at some point and left there. The students took it as a challenge to climb up the outside and stand and swear or gesticulate from the top of it, which was nice. Again, the advice on how best to handle this situation varied but we did have walkie talkies which added to the drama and gave the conflicting advice a new medium through which to travel. Sometimes we were told to walk away, sometimes to try to talk them down and bring them in. I was very careful not to accidentally attach any of these walkie talkies to my pants as that kind of tomfoolery might have been less forgivable at this school. They were really just a placebo anyway, to make us feel as if we had control when the truth was far from it. I was never comfortable with the idea of walking away from students up to no good on a rooftop and I am so glad nobody was hurt.

A well-meaning member of staff had at some point planted a beautiful willow tunnel, perhaps with the idea of attracting wildlife and distracting the students from the container or the fence. They probably never imagined that it would grow into a renewable weaponry source which needed at least 3 members of staff to guard. The students were so quick it was hard to stop them and once a cane of willow had been snapped off and stripped it could cause a great deal of pain before staff could tackle the offender and retrieve it. Once confiscated, the game would begin again, with more students joining in. The worst offenders were a couple of boys who looked very similar, both had names which started with 'K', they could have been called Kai, Kye, Kian, Kyan, Kane, Keiron, I can't remember now, but I used to think of them as the chimney sweep boys, agile, fast, rude and a bit grubby but probably exactly the right size to send up a chimney. They had hard faces which showed that they had felt the cruelty they now dished out and if they smiled it only ever seemed to be at someone else's expense. They appeared to feel no remorse, they never apologised and every day they were the same- hyped up on adrenalin and finding their actions extremely funny no matter what the impact was on the other students. If all this sounds like a bit of a nightmare, I suppose at times it was, but the front-line staff shared a good sense of humour and were genuinely doing their best for the students. Those who had survived the drama and relentless inspections were tired of the constant change and the stigma now associated with the school. They were amazingly resilient people to come to work each day and face the situations they did, in the hope that things were going to get better.

Chapter 15 Make the right choice

T here were cohorts of students who reliably 'made the right choice' and some who succeeded in exams and made good progress. However, one such student unexpectedly 'went into crisis' (we were banned from using the phrase 'melt down') during a maths exam, which surprised everyone. Usually, this young man was solidly reliable, he was heavily built, about six feet tall and appeared more advanced than his years and had never presented any real behavioural issues until that maths exam. With apparently no warning, his paper was flung, his pens and pencils were thrown, and the desk and chair were hurled across the exam room. He was shouting and swearing and for a long time he was inconsolable, completely ruining the exam conditions for everyone else. This was out of character for him and when everything calmed down, it became clear that the cause of the crisis was a black and white line drawing of a packet of crisps, used to illustrate a maths problem.

This student had a serious and apparently uncontrollable crisp phobia and was so upset by the drawing that he couldn't continue with the exam. His teachers had known about the phobia, and in everyday life they made sure nobody entered the room with crisps or talked about crisps and they were careful about taking him out of school in case he saw some crisps, but they couldn't prevent the crisps appearing in an exam paper. In the end the school had to contact the exam board and explain the situation, and everybody agreed that they had never heard of that happening before. I am not sure whether he was granted some 'special circumstances' leniency or not, or whether his poor classmates were given extra time.

Eventually, the mezzanine on the landing outside my classroom became a hazard, Items such as toilet rolls, chairs, school bags, computers and 'wet floor' signs were thrown from it too many times. I secretly worried about how long it would be before someone brought in a vat of boiling oil or a catapult. It was eventually blocked off by a sliding metal screen like the ones used to secure the outside of shops, which made a horribly satisfying noise for the students when chairs were thrown against it. Like a massive percussion instrument, it reverberated loudly across the first floor and down into the dining hall below. Blocking off the gap was a good idea, although it looked a bit prison-like, because it also stopped the students below from trying to throw their food up high enough to go over the top of the glass balcony. If they succeeded, it would end up outside my classroom. It is part of the unwritten job description of teachers to get stuck into cleaning unpleasant things up, so if you believe we sit our desks and teach or mark and are not therefore part of the real world then this view needs to be dispelled, and these brief details of what else might be involved are not pretty.

In primary and nursery school there is often sick, stray poo, wee, snot or nosebleeds to be dealt with, in secondary some of the same applies, though perhaps less often. If you are working with young people with PMLD or SLD the job may become even more personal and although most schools will employ support assistants for intimate care, if you are short staffed then you must help out. Sometimes this has involved changing every piece of a young person's clothing after a stomach upset- if you have had children yourself you may have experienced nappy leakage reaching up to the back of your baby's neck and down their legs to their socks because of the nature of being in a sitting position in a pushchair or car seat. It is the same with older people, it just happens on a larger scale. Often young people will need to keep a supply of spare clothes at school in case this happens and if they are immobile, it happens fairly frequently because of the medication they are often on to keep things inside moving. We also sometimes need to use suction machines to relieve mucus congestion in the mouth- this is a gruesome job and not for the faint hearted. It involves gently moving a plastic straw-like hoover around the inside of the mouth which collects the mucus, sends it down a little tube and deposits it in a canister. Occasionally parents would forget to empty this and the machine would then become quite a disgusting bio hazard of old phlegm. There is also the necessity to look after the personal hygiene needs of young women who have their monthly cycles, if they need help to do this. All of these aspects of the job are 'behind the scenes' but are an essential part of making sure that young peoples' needs are met, and must be done compassionately and respectfully to make sure the dignity of students is not compromised. Sometimes it may be necessary to help out with other non-teacherly jobs too, such as the unblocking of toilets, if the toilet happens to be right next to your classroom and the issue is gradually creeping in your direction. This was almost a daily ritual at the school with the mezzanine, and I couldn't work out whether it was caused by a member of staff or a student. It just became part of my morning routine to mince up somebody else's poo blockage and give it all a good mop.

In an English lesson I was explaining to the students that if they worked hard and passed as many exams as they could then they would have a much better choice of job. One of them asked me if I'd worked hard at school and I replied that I had. He asked me if I'd been to university and again, I said I had. I stupidly still couldn't see where the conversation was going until he laughed and pointed out that it hadn't got me very far- I was spending every day in the same place as they were, only they would never be daft enough to spend their whole lives there. I thought about that, and I still think about it- I am still jumping up when a bell rings, still training my bladder to go for a wee when I am allowed, but I get to unblock toilets and do a whole lot of other unpleasant things too.

In the same lesson we went on to talk about CVs and how they would need to know their own personal information for when they applied for jobs or filled in benefit forms. I had given them all a blank general sort of application form for them to use as a practice and realised towards the end of the lesson that one of the boys had copied his friend's answers word for word. He was happy with this, until I pointed out that if he was applying for benefits then his friend would end up getting his money instead of him. The rest of his class thought that this was hilarious, but he wasn't bothered, he took nothing seriously and as long as he was listening to his favourite song of the moment, which at that time was 'Cheerleader' and talking about girls he fancied, he was happy. I found out a couple of years ago that he has now become a father. I wonder whether he has needed to write any of his personal details down anywhere for that job role.

Chapter 16 Monster

After a while, I figured out that some of the exuberant behaviour from students might be linked to their consumption of energy drinks on their way to school, while at school, and occasionally even during lessons. I went to talk to my leaders, and they supported the idea that we should attempt to ban them from the school premises. Some of the students took it as a personal challenge to 'top load' as many cans of Monster as they could while they were in their taxis, and it was very difficult to police the situation.

I had also been thinking about the chats we would have when they would share their news of the weekend, and decided that a number of them might benefit from a visit from the local drug and alcohol recovery service. I arranged for the Education officer to visit during one of my English lessons and she agreed.

The students were excited, as they always were when there was a new face, and even more excited when they saw that she had brought with her a set of boxes. Each one was divided into little compartments, each compartment containing information about a different drug and a (fake) sample of it. The boxes had Perspex lids to allow students to look at each one and read the information. They contained details of every drug imaginable, many that were familiar to students and a large amount that weren't. Green and cowies (the northeast slag term for ecstasy) were the drugs of choice at this school, but many had witnessed or been involved in some way with coke, and they were open about it. The lady had been in the room for less than ten minutes and had barely started on her drug information talk when all the lids were suddenly off, and the samples were snaffled and hidden down trousers or in inside pockets. It took the rest of the lesson and a great deal of determination to retrieve the samples. I didn't dare ask her to visit again and wasn't sure what to do about their extra-curricular activities. I did ask her to visit my next school however, and when I reminded her that we had met before, she pretended that she didn't remember. I understand that trauma can do that sometimes.

Drugs are nothing new and it is unrealistic to think any secondary school is unaffected by them. Now I teach drugs education and I explain to the young people that it isn't a question of if they will be offered drugs, but when. I was offered ecstasy in my A level art lessons in the early 90's (I declined- preferring snakebite and black, which sounds totally disgusting now) and the use of recreational drugs has exploded since then. Even in the convent there were rumours of shenanigans in the toilets which didn't involve custard and probably needed a whole lot of Hail Marys to put right.

One student was seen hobbling about on the yard, looking shifty, and on closer inspection it turned out he had hidden a nubbin of green in one of his stinking and crusty socks. This student was on a watch list already for bringing a knife into school and every morning he was checked over with a metal detector wand like the ones used in airports. He was a loveable character but had to be watched. He had the potential for physical violence and was built like a boxer- shoulders curved round, neck immobile and disappearing into them and a bit of a defensive squint when he looked up. When he started school in year 7 he was like a feral animal and didn't really attend lessons. He could be heard before he was seen, swearing at the top of his voice as he was marched along the corridor by staff, his feet skipping briskly along the floor. He was small and fair haired, but as he grew, he became like a miniature man very quickly. He was from the traveller community, and was always trading things, offering to get staff a better car or motorbike (if you weren't fussy about it having keys) and most staff found that he was only engaged in lessons which could somehow be related to quadbikes, motorbikes or car trading. As he grew older, his absences from school worried staff who suspected his involvement in 'county lines' as he was an ideal candidate. He was very interested in normal family life and would ask staff what they did at home and listen intently as though the mundane details were fascinating to him. Family life for him was unpredictable and he spent time with older youths who invited him to stay over and play video games, and who knew what else... he was very vulnerable. Trying to educate young people like this is difficult because of their absenteeism. There were so many times over the years that I tried to organise drugs or county lines education for his lesson, but he would be absent on the day it was arranged.

Eventually management decided that behaviour in the school could be better, perhaps someone or something had splatted against those hermetically sealed and soundproofed picture windows which nicely contained the chaos of the dining hall, and they realised something should be done. The fault, it was decided, was the inconsistent attitudes of staff towards incidents of negative behaviour. What a surprise. We were all already 'Team Teach' trained, a programme which enables staff to de-escalate situations to help students to avoid going into crisis. Some of this training involves physical restraint techniques which are only ever used as a very last resort if the student is likely to hurt themselves. Even if the student is likely to hurt someone else a restraint can only be used if the purpose is to stop that student being emotionally hurt by the consequences of their actions against another person (this often refers to the potential of police involvement). This school did not support the use of physical interventions and we were strongly discouraged from using them. In the rare event it was needed, a full report would have to be written up in a large black 'bound and numbered book' in case the student later sued, and the case ended up in court. This meant that staff were afraid to even support students physically, for fear of being accused of not following protocol. Most of the Team Teach training is about circles of danger, body language and understanding the effects of adrenalin. We knew that all behaviour is communication, and we also knew that positive relationships, clear boundaries and consistency of rewards and consequences were what would improve things.

However, a system was introduced which missed out the relationships bit, ignored the fact that our students all responded to things differently and had no clear consistency of consequences. It was decided that all behaviour must be approached and managed in exactly the same way. We were to follow a script and use a set of square cards attached to our lanyards as a visual prompt for the students. Some students did use visual prompts such as 'communicate in print' which converted words into pictures, but others were quite capable of reading and writing. In the event of a lesson malfunction (which it was suggested was never the fault of the student- we had to ask ourselves why our lessons were forcing the students to behave in this way) we had to show the young person the STOP card and tell them clearly to "Stop" whatever the behaviour was. Simple. In the unlikely event that the behaviour continued, we were to carry on through the script and present the flash the cards clearly to the student, until the final card read "serious clause". This was confusing- there was no communicate in print symbol for that one and none of the staff or the students knew what that was. Could we extradite them somewhere far away? Could we ask them to do a thousand press-ups or repaint the classroom? Were we allowed to wash their mouths out with soap or force them to rewrite all the policy documents? There was no serious clause.

Reward trips for the worst offenders were introduced and were increasingly popular. Every week more of the worst offenders from every year group would gather below my classroom window and wait for the 'outward bound' teacher to let them onto the minibus, and they would be off on an adventure. Even using basic psychology, the incentives to offend were great, and the flash card system did not work because we were not dealing with cyborgs.

The way successful teachers deal with negative behaviours is always going to depend on the relationship between the teacher and the student, the teacher will know whether to use humour, choices, reminders, or praise for the positives, know what behaviour to ignore, what the back story is and how to turn that young person around again, which may include stepping back and allowing a different member of staff to take over. It is a delicate matter of diplomacy and compassion. We were admonished publicly in staff meetings if we had been overheard not following the script. One of our leaders found themselves in the awkward position of demonstrating the system one day to a real live student, and this gathered a bit of an audience. I missed it, but I heard through several reliable sources that the situation went like this:

1. Book thrown at senior member of staff.
2. Script loaded, card held up, "STOP" (emotionless face)
3. Book thrown again (different book, hardback this time- a bit heavier).
4. "STOP" (emotionless face)
5. Steps 3-4 followed until the student had gained the skills needed to aim the book and successfully hit the head of the leader. Leader flinching but unmoved.
6. Ridiculous situation continued until stu-

dent became tired of throwing books.

The leader was injured but had apparently acted afterwards as though the whole thing had gone perfectly to plan.

Everyone watching marvelled at how the student had been allowed to continue throwing books for so long and how much his hand-eye coordination had improved.

Chapter 17 Losing my Mojo

I t felt as if pressure was mounting in all directions and behavioural issues were not getting
any better. We were encouraged to fill in an
incident report on 'Behaviour Watch' after every
occurrence of anti-social behaviour, but it was impossible to keep up with them, so this meant we
stayed back after work to try to log all the incidents
that had happened that day, and it was not unusual
for this to take an hour or more. The programme
was intended to be used to track both positive
and negative behaviours, to attempt to see patterns
and possible causes and prevent negative behaviours from happening again. Without warning, and
shortly after the lanyard cards and script had been
introduced, detentions were suddenly banned. I
had put one on the system for an incident of threatening behaviour and suddenly it was gone. I had
promised the young man involved that he would be
having a detention, but he made a special trip to my
room and appeared, grinning, to give me the news
himself that there were now no detentions. He was
over the moon as he had the bonus of the reward
trip to look forward to later in the week (which was
still going ahead.) I was surprised and not delighted

at all. We even had a member of staff who had been given the role of behaviour manager, but she was powerless and could see things getting worse.

Eventually some sort of compromise was reached, and it was decided that if staff insisted on giving students detentions as their choice of 'serious clause' (I still don't know what other options there were) then they would have to supervise the detention themselves. So, if you had a student who had destroyed your lesson, walked over desks and told you that they would like to punch you in the face, you then had to spend your lunchtime alone with them, trying not to end up being punched in the face (or ruining your career by punching them in the face.) If staff thought a student should have an after-school detention, then it was their responsibility to drive them home, alone, in their own car, which was an insane risk to take. So therefore, there were no sanctions unless a member of staff fancied leaving themselves open to accusations or assault.

Assaults on staff were not uncommon, and never, to my knowledge, resulted in staff taking legal action against a student. There was one occasion when a member of staff was alone in a classroom and a student followed her in and seriously assaulted her, when she fell to the floor, he hit her again. She managed to crawl towards the door and push her arm past the threshold so she might be seen by somebody walking down the corridor and luckily another member of staff happened to see her and sought help. This lady was off work for a number of weeks, with a head injury and an injury to her shoulder, which restricted the mobility of her arm for a long while afterwards, not to mention lasting psychological effects.

When I witness assaults or see injuries that are routinely inflicted on staff who work in special schools it strikes me how forgiving the staff are, the 'unconditional positive regard' we have towards pupils goes to the extreme. Staff who work in units providing support for students with severe autism often suffer the most but never seem to complain. Some wear long woolly gloves which reach past their elbows, as this deters students from biting their arms. It doesn't always stop them though, which inevitably results in a trip to hospital for a hepatitis injection. Many staff are spat at from time to time, and injuries from flying furniture or tipped tables are also common. Police officers have the option of applying for compensation if they are spat at, but this is not so in schools. Even in the middle of a global pandemic, we have students who will deliberately spit or cough in the faces of staff and other students. I sometimes wish that the media would visit a real school, not a faked-up version with half a dozen perfectly behaved and polite children. This would help the general public to understand what teachers and support staff must deal with, so that they stop with the teacher bashing. Teachers and support staff do this kind of work because they care, they are trying to help, that's it. There are no expenses claims or mileage allowances, no staff canteen, no lunch hour, no taking or making personal calls: we just try to help the nation's young people and that requires 100% effort all day..

Recently I was watching an episode of Police Interceptors, and an officer had been called to attend a shop where a youth was behaving unsociably. They called for back-up and other officers went to assist. They were equipped with tasers, pepper spray, handcuffs and I don't know what else, and there were several officers dealing with the one youth. It struck me that in a school setting we are often in potentially dangerous situations with the same youths, in larger numbers and have no way of defending ourselves. Physical interventions follow very strict protocols and are in any case only ever used to protect the student involved. The truth is that it can be a dangerous job.

My mojo was inevitably disappearing, this was a challenging workplace and because I was officially an annoying and inferior member of the middle management I had kissed goodbye to my rights to a work-life balance. I would be constantly bombarded with emails inviting me to immediate and urgent after school meetings (most nights), while my personal children waited an hour away and had no idea when I would be home. This was not easy as a single parent, especially when I would have a pile of schoolwork to complete before the next day. Some of these meetings were undeniably important, others involved us taking part in a lengthy, expensive and slightly odd personality analysis which eventually produced a thick booklet telling us all about ourselves. It was interesting in the same way that the social media quizzes are which tell you of your spirit animal, what cocktail you should be and what your future holds if you identify with a particular sponge scourer. The journey to work was becoming less fun too, if I was held up and didn't make a certain roundabout by 7:45 I would be stuck in traffic for an extra half hour. One morning I managed to be nearly two hours late for work- a total travelling time of three hours. I could have been most of the way to London if I'd got on a train.

My job role was also shifting, I had been employed to oversee literacy and communication in the Primary department, but my Secondary counterpart had been encouraged to leave part way through the year. He may have annoyed some of the leadership team with his laissez-faire attitude and dry sense of humour. He would routinely arrive late to meetings because he needed to warm up a Spanish tortilla in his microwave, and he would then defiantly sit

back and enjoy the steaming potato and egg con-
coction at the conference table. He savoured every
bite. I don't think that was the only reason he left,
but the result was that I had his work to do as
well as my own, which made me responsible for all
things English across the school, which was a big
responsibility the way things were. We had made
some headway with sorting out baseline assessments and we were tracking progress, which was
good in some of the calmer classes. We also introduced 'Fresh start' which was a literacy programme
designed for secondary aged students who struggled with reading. In the primary department we
sorted out more appropriate 'read write ink' groups
and staff were trained to deliver it.

The inspectors kept on coming, but they said they
were pleased with what they had seen happening
in the school, it was all excellent (from behind the
safety of the glass walls in the management area.)
This was good news, the new management were
turning around the dodgy reputation of the school
and things were apparently on the up, which was
nice. The school had always had a good reputation,
before the unpleasantness, and it seems to me that
most schools naturally go through cycles of success. One Friday morning they asked for volunteers
to do an extra lunchtime duty, so thinking there
must have been an unforeseen emergency, I went
and did my half hour outside and then came in to

supervise the riot in the dining hall for the next half. Lunchtime duty in the hall was always a nightmare, there would be fights to break up or prevent, energy drinks to confiscate and language to monitor. On this occasion it turned out we were doing this extra duty so that our leaders could relax and celebrate the success of the latest inspection with a well-deserved and lovely buffet lunch. We watched the caterers carry the trays of goodies into the inner sanctum, while those of us who had selflessly volunteered to cover the extra duties, got no lunch at all.

One night it all became too much, I had promised my children I wouldn't be too late, and I thought I'd better check my emails one last time after completing 'behaviour watch' before logging off and gathering my belongings together. Sitting there boldly and unapologetically in my inbox was another random meeting announcement scheduled for that night, and my brain exploded. My lovely teaching assistant, the kind and patient Mrs R was aware that the stress and the travelling time was beginning to get to me and that I felt torn between home and work. She joined forces with the caretaker and together they bundled up my stuff, opened the emergency fire exit (so I wouldn't have to run the gauntlet of the glass inner management sanctum downstairs) and shoved me out of it. "Run!" they said "Run to your car and don't look back!" and I did. The next day I pretended that I hadn't seen the email.

Chapter 18 All Change

I had been in my new house for about a year, the children and I had dug a pond, laid a patio and installed some guinea pigs, when we were invited to move in with a lovely man who I had known vaguely for about 15 years, we had become friends more recently and occasionally went to the pub to watch a skiffle band. His company was easy and he was kind, so I said yes, although I had solemnly vowed after leaving my first husband that I would never get involved with anyone ever again. Moving in with him meant that the travelling time to work was even further increased, and I knew I couldn't carry on much longer.

There were nine of us living together when we first moved in, and I hadn't appreciated how tricky it could be to 'blend families'. After a while though, some of his adult children left home (I like to think it wasn't because we moved in) and we were a less freakishly large family. When a closer job came up at an 'outstanding' secondary school for students with additional needs I knew I would have to apply. A couple of colleagues who worked with me had previously worked there and spoke about what an amazing school it was. There were two jobs going, they needed a teacher for the PMLD students and another for MLD students, so I decided to apply for both. I rang the school and asked if I could go for a visit, and they arranged an after-school visit on a Friday afternoon. When I got there the car park was empty, which was a good sign and showed that staff were obviously comfortable with the concept of being at home in the evenings. Unfortunately, the day had been particularly demanding, and I have never been blessed with a sophisticated (or even particularly tidy) appearance. The head greeted me, and I apologised for looking as if I had been dragged through a hedge backwards. I felt the need to explain- I had been in a hedge that day to retrieve a student but I had gone in voluntarily. I thought that was important to clarify.

My friend, Mrs W from work was also applying for the PMLD job and as I said earlier, she was excellent. A few weeks later we found ourselves waiting together in the entrance lobby of this new school to be interviewed. The vibes were good, I always think you can tell the ethos of a school pretty quickly and the staff who went past us seemed happy enough. The PMLD interview was first and after every answer I told them that my friend would be so much better at it than me, which was true, I couldn't lie. She got the job and I was genuinely pleased for her, one of us had got out and that was something. The head advised me that my interview strategy needed looking at, but if I stayed around the interviewees for the general teacher job would be arriving soon. I wondered briefly if I had shot myself in the foot and should have maybe tried harder to compete with my friend, but I believed in her far more than myself and I couldn't fake it. Back in the interview room I had to talk them through how I would do a maths lesson, which I remember involved being outside, turning students into multilink cubes and had something to do with post it notes. Luckily, I got the job and was happy to let go of the management role to be a 'normal' teacher again (if such a thing exists).

We worked our notice until the Christmas, both Mrs W and I felt sadness at leaving the students and our colleagues, and I felt as if I was letting some of them down. It turned out that a number of the staff had secured jobs elsewhere so on the last day it felt like the end of an episode for many of us. Sadly, I wasn't allowed to accompany the students on their end of term reward trip- I had to stay in school to rewrite some student reports in which I had been too honest. I thought I had phrased my reports very positively, but they were apparently not positive enough. This turned out to be my 'serious clause' and the idea that I was the one who had finally been given a detention and had missed the reward trip on the last day was very funny.

It was just as well that I had changed jobs to be nearer to home as the week before Christmas we had some devastating news about my youngest son, who was then 10. He had been poorly for a while, complaining of severe rib pain and he had been treated for pneumonia in the autumn. The week before Christmas, they repeated a chest x-ray at the request of my mum, who is always more assertive than me, and then we went home. Later that day the consultant rang me and asked if we could go straight back to the hospital, but he wouldn't say why over the phone. I had a horrible sinking feeling as I started the long drive back, and they didn't keep us waiting once we arrived. The nurses kindly played the giant plastic version of connect four with my son, while we went into the consultation room with the doctor. I remember clearly the doctor's face, the chairs, the expression on my mum's face and I think if you have ever been in a similar situation, you will understand that the small details of these moments stay with you forever. The doctor looked extremely concerned as he explained that the x-ray showed that one of my son's ribs was missing, there was just a cloudy dark fuzziness, a gap where it should have been on the x-ray. He gently explained that the only thing that destroys bone in that way was cancer, and that an oncology appointment had already been made for the following morning. The words cancer and oncology are difficult to hear or accept, and the worst scenario is if it is in relation to a diagnosis for your child. He gave us no other possibilities- it was just a matter now of discovering what type of cancer it was and how it could be treated. It was as though everything slowed down and became unreal, we were suddenly treading a different path, numbly trying to understand what would happen next while the rest of the world were out Christmas shopping.

The RVI were nothing short of brilliant. They made a huge, cheerful fuss of him and because it was Christmas, he was given armfuls of Christmas presents which had been donated to the Children's oncology ward, which really helped to distract him from the countless blood tests and procedures. Fourteen x-rays of his body were taken to start with, and I always intended to buy the CD so that we could reconstruct his skeleton for his bedroom wall, but in all the drama and stress it never happened. He had CAT scans and an MRI and my ex-husband and I were ushered into side rooms every few hours to discuss their findings. One of the young doctors looked as though she was close to tears, and I remember I felt sorry that she was upset- while we were still numb. They talked about a 'lesion' and a tumour but nobody could tell me how big the tumour was and it was all very confusing. We had been told to expect that it was probably Ewing's sarcoma but as the days went on, we were told by one consultant that there was a small chance it was something extremely rare called Langerhan's Cell Histiocytosis. In that case, the news could be a whole lot better. LCH is a type of cancer which can still be fatal, but the RVI is a world leader in gathering information about this disease, and if you had to pick a cancer, LCH in somewhere other than your head is probably the best option.

On Christmas Eve he was transferred to another hospital and they did a biopsy, scooping out the mush that was left where his rib should have been. We were later sent home to enjoy Christmas, the wait for the biopsy results was to be an agonising ten days. It is odd, but part of me didn't mind the ten days. We were in the capable hands of the RVI, and while I didn't know the diagnosis, I still had hope. That Christmas was surreal, but we stayed very positive, managed to have fun and appreciated every moment. My mum struggled with it, and wasn't as subtle as I think she imagined herself to be, she seemed to need to take photos of him every few seconds like an emotional member of the paparazzi. I had been told by the consultant to prepare him for the possibility that he would lose his hair if he needed treatment, and this was too much. He had remained strong and cheerful up to that point but the thought of wearing the woolly hat that we'd bought tipped him over the edge and he was upset. Meanwhile mum had contacted every church in the local area to have him added to their prayer lists.

I had to start my new job in the January not know-ing what the future was going to look like but my new management were very supportive, they hadn't expected me to go in to work at all and allowed me as much time off as I needed for ap-pointments. Eventually, we were called back to face up to the results of the biopsy and we were told that he definitely had LCH. It was extraordinarily good news, the chances had been so small, the hope so slim. It was like winning the lottery only a mil-lion times better. We were told that the bone had turned to mush because some of his cells had mu-tated and become destructive. Until very recently, the treatment would have been chemotherapy, but research conducted in the previous year or so had indicated that miraculously, it may not necessary. They believed that just by taking a biopsy and inter-fering with the rogue cells which had destroyed the rib might just kick start them into rebuild-ing it again. This was innovative, not guaranteed, and his condition was monitored closely to find out whether it would work. We were incredulous; it was truly amazing to have suddenly been given such a positive prognosis. The chances of it being LCH were tiny, and the chances of it being some-where as relatively harmless as a rib even smaller. He had frequent repeat x-rays and sure enough, the rib grew back, stronger and better than ever before.

He believed himself to be Wolverine, with super-magical regenerating and healing powers.

Eventually, the oncology appointments reduced to every six months and then annually, at Christmas. Whatever had been going on in our personal lives, those visits to the children's oncology ward, especially at Christmas put everything sharply into perspective. It was always like hitting a reset button, feeling the raw emotion and seeing the reality of what many families were going through was there in front of us, and it wasn't easy to witness. Every year we take presents for other children who might find themselves unexpectedly in ward 14 at Christmas, knowing that we must be the luckiest of all and feeling incredibly thankful.

Chapter 19 Keep your Head Down

For the first couple of years at my next school I taught a mixture of students with PMLD and MLD, I kept my head down and watched and listened, which I think is always a good way to start a new job. The PMLD students were supported by experienced staff who knew the students well, so again, I watched how they ran things. I was with them for whole days rather than part sessions and eventually I began to relax and enjoy it, although it wasn't teaching as I knew it. In the same way that nursery or foundation aged children learn through play, we provided concrete experiences for them. A big difference between nursery and teaching PMLD students was that the experiences needed to be brought to the students and many needed help to participate. It was a very personal way of teaching, and all the intimate and medical needs of the students also had to be attended to throughout the day. This meant a completely different routine for each student- their schedules were displayed on the wall so that staff could keep track. Everything was recorded including bowel habits, urination frequency and even volume. The day was punctuated frequently by the need to administer meds or change the position of a student, to help with personal care, sort out tube feeds or help with meals.

It felt more like nursing than teaching. Some students went to the dining room for meals, and staff would need to help them to choose appropriate dishes, add a clip on ledge around the plate to keep the food in and stand the plate on a rubber mat to stop it slipping about. Some students could feed themselves with support while others needed feeding. I was helping a student with her dinner one lunchtime and my mind drifted momentarily. Unfortunately, in that moment I scooped the excess yoghurt from the front of my young person's bib and ate it myself. It's the kind of repulsive behaviour you might do in the privacy of your own home with your own babies. I looked around the noisy dining room- nobody had seen me, I'd got away with it. That spoonful of slathery, secondhand yoghurt was the only thing to pass my lips that lunchtime, I lost my appetite after that.

Meds were administered by our school nurse, a long suffering but nevertheless cheerful lady (wild on a night out) who was permanently on call and could always be seen speed walking about the school with her supplies. We were trained to time the length of any fits and to give epilepsy meds if necessary, use epipens and administer adrenalin. We used the hydro pool weekly to give the students a chance to stretch their muscles as part of their physiotherapy requirements, which involved helping them to change and often using a hoist to lower them into the pool. The temperature in the pool room was always set at Club Tropicana Hot, so the physical side of hoisting and changing students was exhausting and staff always looked as if they had done a difficult shift in a Marrakesh hammam afterwards. (I say that with confidence having endured a hammam in Marrakesh) Some students also benefitted from rebound therapy, which involved an enormous trampoline, lots of fun bouncing games and other more specific and technical things. I wasn't trained to do this and it's a good thing as my motion sickness is so extreme, I once very nearly threw up in a pedalo in Corfu. We also had a sensory room, where the students could relax, take part in their prescribed physio exercises and interact with the colour changing lights and sensory equipment.

Day to day, we tried to make life as interesting as possible, we introduced new materials and experiences as well as repeating familiar routines and sensory stories. Some of the equipment that the students had access to was cutting edge- one student had an 'eye gazer' machine which allowed them to track images on a screen and communicate through tiny movements of their eyes. This school was happy to support whatever training we wanted so I collected a raft of CPD certificates for various things and also decided to do the Midas training so that I could drive the minibus. This was brilliant, and meant that after the ordeal of operating the tail lifts, tying down the wheelchairs in line with the necessary protocols and making sure we were fully prepared, we could take students out for a morning or an afternoon. Longer than that was impossible as there were no suitable toileting facilities with hoists. We explored all over the local area, but the students enjoyed the simple things, even the bus ride was the highlight for some. Years later one of these students would still beam whenever he saw me, and do his sign for 'bus'. We would smell the fresh bread in the supermarket, watch the neon fish darting about in illuminated fish tanks in the pet shop and feel the different textures of fabric in wheelchair friendly clothes shops.

I was always very careful when parking the bus, but I didn't always follow the rules of the car parks. At least I never crashed it- unlike a hungry colleague who decided on a last-minute McDonalds drive through and ended up causing some damage driving through the height barrier, which apparently was considerably lower than the bus. Sometimes I parked across a number of bays to make sure we had enough space for the students to board the tail lift, after a couple of situations where we had been hemmed in. I felt the same irritation at these times as I'd felt when my daughter was young and told she should test her blood in the toilets or not inject in public. Being with people who have additional needs, whether they are breast feeding babies or adults with disabilities, makes you aware of difficult it can be just to do normal things without attracting attention, and sadly, sometimes how intolerant people can be. Some supermarket cafes were openly welcoming to our little group, others were hostile. Often we wanted to allow students with particular dietary needs to eat their own packed lunch while others bought a snack from the cafe, but this mix and match scenario sadly wasn't tolerated everywhere. We always tried to encourage students to communicate with staff in cafés to order a drink or snacks, if they were able to, and used PECS cards (picture exchange communication system) where they were helpful.

The paperwork now involved in taking students off site, even for half an hour, is enough to deter even the most enthusiastic of teachers. It takes almost an entire day to gather together all the necessary paperwork as every single part of the trip needs a specific risk assessment. This includes getting on or off the bus, the bus journey and every place visited at the destination. In addition to that, if you are taking students with any medical needs, moving and handling plans, behaviour plans or risk assessments of their own, all that information needs to be added to decide whether it is safe for them (and the general public) to leave the school. Then there are the letters to parents and their consent forms, which are often filled in incorrectly with the wrong mobile number or no mobile number at all, and a whole host of forms which justify why you are taking students off site, what the educational benefits will be, how many students of which gender and year group and documents for staff to sign to say they are happy to lose their job if anything goes wrong. When all the documents are complete they are considered by a senior leader and sent to County Hall to be approved. On top of that there is the mini bus to book and school meals to cancel or lunches to order and if you forget to do either of the last two you will end up being extremely unpopular with the kitchen staff and may as well look for another job. Staff must make sure that they take medication with them for those students either routinely given meds in school or who need them kept in school for emergencies, as well as the first aid kit, sick bowls and usual paraphernalia. Some of the documents must go with the group leader on the trip, others must be left behind in the office. What must never be left behind in the office are the meds needed for the trip, the emergency contact numbers or any of the students themselves.

However, it was definitely worth the hassle and stress to complete the paperwork needed to take my group out, they loved it and gained so much from the experience. Measuring progress for PMLD students is necessary, in just the same way as it is for all students, but their achievements are broken down into very small steps, and might include things like making eye contact, vocalising a greeting or expressing happiness with a smile. For some students however, progress follows a different course and if they have a degenerative condition, we often see skills being lost rather than gained (this is worth remembering, school inspectors!) These students, all of whom had very complex needs, were well looked after by the staff and I sometimes think that PMLD support staff and teachers aren't given the credit they deserve, even keeping these students safe, healthy and happy is a challenge. It wasn't my forte but now that I have been involved in working with students with profound and multiple learning difficulties, I understand how difficult it can be both physically and emotionally and also how rewarding it is. Mrs W is still excelling in this department. I also have the greatest respect for parents of children with profound difficulties as that is another level of parenting altogether.

The days when I wasn't working with the students with PMLD I worked with students with moderate learning difficulties teaching all sorts of subjects including maths, ICT, science and PE, although I think in ICT the transfer of knowledge was from them to me rather than from me to them. The students at this school were similar to my previous school on paper and all had a range of different additional needs, but they were not as raw and spirited somehow. They were generally less jumpy and unpredictable, fewer of them were interested in pushing boundaries quite as openly as the students were from the other school. Maybe this was because the catchment area was slightly different- more villages and small towns and less students from the cities in Tyne and Wear or the economically disadvantaged coastal areas. It was also probably because this school was stable and had been ticking along very nicely with the same reliable and competent staff who hadn't been tortured by the system. There were clear boundaries, and the students were well aware of the consequences of their actions. This does not mean that behaviour was always excellent- the students still had additional needs and therefore many struggled with regulating their behaviour in different circumstances. Rewards were used as an incentive here- they could be accumulated for a McDonalds at the end of the term or cashed in immediately for prizes, and most students responded well to this. We also had a Behaviour Support Unit, ready and waiting to step in and escort repeat offenders away so that lessons could continue.

Not having a classroom to call home was difficult, and I would have to haul my stuff around school all day, trying not to leave anything behind anywhere. Carrier bags weren't frowned upon here, at least if they were nobody frowned openly, and I think everybody was far too busy to notice me and my dozens of bags. Teaching so many different subjects and moving around school was difficult to organise, particularly for science or maths lessons when resources were needed, and I felt as if I didn't know anybody well enough to ask for help sourcing things. I needed to just get on with it, deal with what was going on in my personal life and do as good a job as possible. I inherited a tricky year 11 class for science and was told that the topic they needed to cover next was periods and contraception. Over the years you realise that in teaching you can be asked to step into any situation at any time and the main thing is to show no fear. 'OK' I said, and planned for my first meeting with this group. The other thing you realise eventually is that some of your colleagues are likely to get a kick out of testing new staff in the same way as the students do. I am still not convinced that periods and contraception were on the syllabus to be taught in exactly the same week as I started but there are few perks in teaching, so I don't blame them for trying to have some fun with me. Most of this year 11 group were boys, a couple were lively (which is code for disruptive) and one of them could end up extremely challenging if you were unlucky enough to teach him the lesson before his next dose of ADHD meds. My lesson was, of course, the lesson before his ADHD meds. I made myself into a physical representation of the female reproductive system which freaked them out enough for me to have their absolute attention. My arms became fallopian tubes and from my hand-ovaries I loudly popped an imaginary egg, demonstrating the monthly turn taking by popping an egg next from the other hand. They got it, and my alternative but down to earth methods won them over. Every now and then when they were least expecting it I would stand behind one of them and mime a kind of Mexican wave ovulation, long after the topic was over, just because it made them laugh.

My first lesson observation at this school was with the same group. Other staff thought this was a dodgy choice, the fact that we even had a choice about which classes to be observed teaching seemed amazingly generous to me. In my previous job we had been observed continuously with no notice so I felt that choosing an easier group was somehow a cop out. We were looking at blood, so I planned to recap the position of the major organs and then to create a blood mixture with the students so that the lesson was as practical as possible. The life-sized organs had been drawn and laminated and all my blood ingredients were ready-cheerios for red blood cells, mini marshmallows for white blood cells, red and yellow food colouring for plasma etc. The first part of the lesson needed audience participation- I needed a student volunteer to lie on the floor so that I could draw around them and they could then discuss what each organ did and place them in the right position inside the body shape. It was all going well- the group seemed enthusiastic but when I asked for a volunteer there was unnatural silence. No amount of coaxing would entice any of these young people on to the floor where they could be drawn around and I suppose in hindsight that is a good thing. I am forever telling them to listen to their bodies and refuse to take part in anything weird that doesn't feel right, so this was exactly the kind of situation I had warned them about. For the purposes of my observation however it was a problem. In the end it was clear that the only option was for me to be the one lying on the floor while they drew my outline. I vividly remember lying there looking up at the ceiling, gabbling enthusiastically but wishing it was all over, my class peering down at me while my deputy head took notes from somewhere in the room. Yet again I was reminded somehow of childbirth.

The rites of passage had to be gone through and that's just how it is if you move to a new school, whether you're a student or a teacher. One of my favourite people, working as an LSA, was terrifying when I first met her, I took a 'Family Group' session which involved a selection of students from year

7 to sixth form, brought together to have fun and learn about 'Right Respecting Schools' activities. I entered the room and with her usual cool attitude she sat down, folded her arms and told me to 'crack on'. I knew none of these students, I made mistakes, made them laugh and somehow passed her test. She has been a good friend ever since and can be relied upon to tell you how it is- no frills, just honesty, which is a rare quality. With well over a hundred staff, all brought together by a common goal, you get more than an average number of excellent people. Many share the kind of dry, dark sense of humour you might find in hospital settings- not everything we face is easy so humour is needed. Other members of staff bring silliness- practical jokes and fun nights out. There are cliques and politics the same as any workplace but the advantage of such a large staff is the richness of experience and ideas that people bring with them, and there is always somebody to talk to.. in theory anyway- and if there was time.

Chapter 20 Sex, Drugs and Birth Control

After a couple of years being a nomad around the school, teaching anything from maths to science, ICT or PE, the PSHE teacher secured a job somewhere exotic and sunny, and I pleaded to take on the role. I felt as if all my life experiences could actually be useful, and I could squeeze some valuable positives from them. It also meant that I had a base, a classroom to call my own and somewhere to leave my cuppa soups. Luckily for me they agreed and the following year I was ready to go, my new tutor group were welcomed, and I had a fabulous LSA to work with.

One of the strengths of this school was that PSHE was taken seriously, and each class was timetabled a lesson each week to learn about all the vital stuff not covered in other subjects. This now includes work on healthy relationships, grooming, exploit-ation, healthy living, finances including debt and tax, politics, mental wellbeing and a host of other massively important topics.

My LSA, Mrs R and I, decided to start with this group as we meant to go on- firm but fair, with plenty of additional incentives to be the best they could be. Part of our plan was to create a display to showcase their achievements, and we thought a safe theme to engage them with would be monsters. We started them off with a nice warm up 'get to know you' type activity where they could create a monster or mythical beast of their own which would carry all the reward points we hoped they were going to accumulate each week. Things were going well and the class were all settled with paper and pens, I decided they were still young enough to do the whole primary drama thing- everyone close your eyes and visualise your monster... I got carried away- helping their imaginations spark into life, (or at least that was the plan) what colour it could be? how did it feel? was it hairy or scaly? Slimy or cold, like a fish? Did it have wings? Or arms or paws? Did it have testicles? At that point I knew that what had come out of my mouth wasn't right. I knew that testicles wasn't the word I had intended to say. I couldn't think at that moment what a testicle was or why it was so wrong but then it dawned on me. I'd been aiming for tentacles and testicles had appeared. I looked around the room. Some of the students had opened an eye and were nervously glancing around them, wondering whether they had imagined what I'd just said. Mrs R, usually so utterly professional, looked at me with horror and then started to laugh, and then all the students started to giggle. I had well and truly blown the whole 'Don't smile till Christmas' nonsense with this lot.

I had already had to teach sex education in science with that year 11 class and I had previously taught all about puberty with primary school pupils. At the convent, my sex education teaching had been a bit sketchy, focussing on the miracle of conception and conveniently missing out on the actual sex part. Less than 5 years after leaving the convent I was at an antenatal appointment with my fourth child and to my horror I recognised one of my ex-pupils sitting there heavily pregnant. I felt personally responsible, and determined that I would do a better job now that I was meant to be teaching it across the school.

I thought it only right to ask for more training, in case anything had changed, so I went to see the manager in charge of sending staff on CPD courses. He had an extremely dry sense of humour and liked to make people squirm. Despite his commanding presence he was well respected by staff, although sometimes it was difficult to find a moment to speak with him. When I did eventually manage to catch him, it was an awkward conversation, he asked if I understood how condoms worked and then asked me what more I needed to know. It was impossible to decide whether he was joking or not and most of my conversations with him left me feeling like an idiot. This feeling lasted for a number of years until I got used to his sense of humour. Of course, he let me do whatever training I wanted, he just needed to know that I wasn't looking for excuses to be out of school. Eventually, our relationship culminated in him offering me some of his private stash of salmon jerky and I felt as though he was now ambivalent towards me, which was a great improvement and I felt very honoured in that moment. He was also the member of the leadership team who dealt with staff absences, a genius move which meant that nobody dared to have a duvet day because the stress of a conversation with him at 7:30 would be far too much of an ordeal to make it worth it.

Over time, my tutor group morphed from quite a happy, easy going bunch into a very tricky collection of young men, with a reputation across the school. This was because both the girls and all of the quieter students were moved out and others were moved in, so that students of a similar ilk could be together in one group. Of 11 students, 9 had risk assessments for challenging or violent behaviour. Somebody must have had faith that we could cope, either that or it was an attempt to move us on... However, as my tutor in Cumbria had wisely said many years earlier 'Whoever said life was meant to be easy?' A few of these boys had a risk assessment which recommended staff were not alone with them, which made things even more difficult when regular support staff were absent as we all depended on those relationships and the continuity they provided. There were many times with this group that I needed to draw on my previous experience and show no outward signs of stress. They could all be difficult in their own ways, and having so many of them in one group was challenging. They were trying to establish a pecking order, so the dynamics were constantly shifting and there always seemed to be somebody with their knuckles bandaged or their hand in a cast. Usually they hit the walls, which luckily were mainly plaster board. Twice a day when I was sitting at the computer taking the register, I had one student who would routinely stand next to me and punch at the side of my head, just stopping short of making contact. He never did it, despite me calmly pointing out that I might get a couple of weeks off work if he did.

I wanted to do the best job possible, so I jumped on board with every new project, training or initiative going and this included joining the 'Sex Ed Commission'. In an attempt to reduce the number of teenage pregnancies in the county, the commission was going to provide CPD and individual support to schools in developing their RSE provision (relationships and sex education) and also give each school money for resources. I had inherited some resources, but they were very disturbing, and I had hidden them in the walk-in cupboard at the back of my classroom. They included two child sized dolls, which could stand independently but were hand stitched and soft bodied. They were indisputably mini adults, with terrifying faces and lust crazed eyes. If you dared to look beneath their clothes, it was the stuff of nightmares. Old Mrs Geppetto had furnished them with generous wads of luxuriously thick black furry body hair, and had used the type of fabric that would be more at home on a toy panther or bear. They boasted oversized and unapologetic genitals, boldly visible beneath their creepy underwear. I researched them and found that they would have been expensive so even if I had thought of a way of disposing of their bodies, I couldn't have justified it. I couldn't ever imagine a lesson where they would do anything other than scar the young people for life.

However, there was something far worse. I was shown this other 'visual aid' by my predecessor before he left the country to start a new life, and while he was showing it to me he admitted that he had only used it once. It lurked in the bottom drawer of the filing cabinet, it's modesty covered by a tea towel. It was made from some kind of soft rubber- I didn't investigate enough to see if it was latex as I didn't want to risk an allergic reaction to it. The explanations involved didn't bear thinking about. It was basically a life sized model of the female pelvic region, with a lift off stomach hatch so that the 3D reproductive organs inside could be seen, a bit like a weird version of the 70's game 'Operation'. It could never be used as a teaching aid though, because the external parts were so realistic looking they were distracting, and it felt morally wrong somehow to be exposed to them. If there had been an equally graphic male version it might have been more acceptable, but I decided against writing it into my lesson plans, and instead, just put the tea towel back over it. I admit that sometimes I ask colleagues if they would mind getting me something from that drawer just to see their reaction and it never fails to surprise them. Recently, this item has been borrowed, and returned in a somewhat violated condition. I have felt that the missing pubic hair and general stickiness of it should be reported to somebody, that ignoring it makes me guilty of failing to report a sex crime, but I am not sure where it would get me. Instead, I have just returned it to the draw and gently placed the tea towel back over the top of it.

Also in the cupboard were more standard props, bags of different types of condoms and condom demonstrators in different flesh tones, plus a purple one- I'm not sure why that had been ordered, but it was a cheerful looking thing. Two much more useful items could be described as fuzzy felt reproductive organ wall hangings, his and hers.

These were great as the bits could be moved around to help to explain things, although the sperm ducts would often end up in a tangle. Once the penis was snatched by a 'lively' student who ran around the classroom hitting people on the head with it. I would have forgotten about that lesson completely if it wasn't for another student mentioning it at parents' night. I was baffled when he told his mum and dad that his friend had stolen my penis and hit him on the head with it, until the next day when I vaguely remembered the incident. At the time, I just had to smile politely at his parents and pretend it was all fine.

The CPD training was extensive, and I attended everything on offer as the cost of replacing me with a cover teacher had been met by the commission. Some of it was really good, I learned a great deal and felt empowered by it. Some of it was surprisingly frank- they did a thorough job of preparing us for any kind of awkward question. However, some of the training on sexuality and gender identity was extreme- one training provider suggested we banish any gender specific words such as female or male, and use the terms 'menstruator' and 'nonmenstruator' to refer to people instead. The staff who attended these training sessions were all open minded and the type of lovely people who would hate to be politically incorrect or offensive. However, as I looked around the room, I could see confusion on all their faces. Many of us worked in schools with students who had additional needs. For these students rebranding the genders in terms of who might or might not be menstruating would be an absolute nightmare. In some SLD classes it is necessary to start with reminding students that people are usually born as boys or girls, before starting on anything to do with puberty or reproduction. The interesting thing was that for almost an entire morning we all sat and listened, and for ages nobody said anything. However, as soon as one person spoke up and questioned the wisdom of this advice, everyone else joined in and eventually they admitted that it might not be appropriate to go down this road in all settings. It is unusual, in my experience, for secondary teachers to keep quiet when they are in a training session if they don't agree with something, but the fear of being seen discriminatory was enough to silence everybody for a while.

I had noticed years earlier that there might be a difference in behaviour and attitude between primary and secondary teachers, when I went to a training session run for staff from both school settings. We were all in a big hall, in groups of six or eight gathered around circular tables, some teachers had come with colleagues, others alone. At one point we were directed to get up from our seats and move to a table where we knew nobody, to do the next task. This caused a polarised reaction in the room, primary teachers generally jumped up enthusiastically and immediately moved to a different table, greeting their unknown colleagues with a cheerful smile and wasting no time in introducing themselves. Secondary teachers, in contrast, generally muttered something offensive or militant under their breath and refused to move anywhere, hunkering down even more firmly where they were. I don't think either attitude is wrong, it just made me smile and I don't know if it's caused by a difference in initial teacher training, personality types or experience. I was trained to teach primary children and therefore usually do as I am told and tend to approach things with a pre-determined and even mindlessly enthusiastic attitude, as that is what has always been expected.

I was reading an article recently where somebody questioned why job ads for teaching roles always ask for 'enthusiastic' and 'highly motivated' applicants. It argued that being expected to 'go the extra mile' and doing so much unpaid overtime leads to burn-out. The writer pointed out that this isn't expected in other job roles, nobody wants a highly motivated and enthusiastic dentist or pilot, people just want them to be able to do their job. Often in training sessions, teachers and support staff are asked to do things that are awkward, embarrassing, cringe-worthy or pointless and most people do take part because of peer pressure and a desire to get it over with. In one of my Sex Ed CPD sessions, we were rounding up at the end and the trainer asked if we could share a sign with the group that showed that provision in our settings was improving, just to finish off with. Eager to go home, I grinned, and with a flourish I showed them all a big double thumbs up gesture. Everyone stared, 'No' she said calmly, 'tell me ways in which your RSE teaching has improved, what signs have you seen?'.

My RSE teaching was going OK, The Sex Ed commission had helped me to write a detailed and comprehensive action plan and all the CPD I had done meant that my subject knowledge was sound and I was not easily embarrassed. If I had a smartypants student who tried to ask me difficult questions just to see if I would squirm, I would give complete and detailed answers which generally wiped the smiles from their faces. There was only one student who ever surprised me- he was y7 and had joined the school in the summer term just as we were starting the topic. I always went through the usual protocols before beginning the topic; I sought parental permission, provided an 'anonymous questions' box by the door of the classroom and established a set of 'ground rules' written together with each class. During our first lesson together this new year 7 student put his hand up and asked me what a 'butt plug' was, and at that I drew the line.

I was happy to answer any questions that I

thought were age appropriate and apart from that year 7 question, (which I thought was inappropriate considering a recap of puberty was shocking enough for them) the ethos in the room meant that students were usually comfortable enough to ask anything. Part of my role was to make sure that students knew what to do in the event of an 'accident' in contraceptive terms and I made sure that both the boys and the girls knew how to use condoms properly, using the condom 'demonstrator'. Twice during these lessons my deputy head walked in and never batted an eyelid, even when one class wanted to try to do it blindfolded. It was more awkward when a potential student and their family was being shown around the school and ended up with more of an insight than they expected- the timing couldn't have been worse. The classroom door burst open and there they stood, just as I was holding the glistening purple condom demonstrator aloft at the front of the class. I was celebrating the achievement of a pupil who had applied the condom perfectly and was showing them all how well it had been fitted. I fleetingly saw the horror on the faces of all the family members before the door was promptly closed again.

I received so many interesting questions (and quite random statements) in the questions box that it kept me entertained every summer for years. Some of them said things like 'How many is it?' or

'How do you tell if you like someone?' or 'Fish have babies' as well as the odd rambling heart felt teenage problem-page type letter. One of these expressed genuine anxiety because the student had discovered they had a strong sexual attraction towards dragons, and they didn't want their mum to know. This situation needed tackling as the young person involved was so troubled it was causing uncharacteristic outbursts of anger. I took them into my room and gently broached the subject and I admit that it was a pretty weird conversation. I reassured them that if it was not causing anyone any harm then it was Ok for it to stay a private matter, and that they could come and talk to me anytime if they felt stressed about it. I was really freestyling and hoping for the best, but it seemed to work as the young person was much calmer and happier afterwards. I however, will never look at dragons in the same way again, but each to their own.

I had another student who would stay behind after every lesson to ask me a very serious personal question about one thing or another. He was an intelligent and sensitive young man with ASC, and he was empathetic to others to the extreme, which is not usually a trait associated with autism. This young man would become very emotional or angry if we discussed injustice, he physically felt the pain of discrimination felt by different minority groups and had a deep interest in politics. His personal questions centred around his confused sexuality, although sometimes he would also throw in a question about Brexit. He wasn't absolutely sure he fancied girls. That was fine I said, and reassured him that he was allowed to feel attracted to boys or girls and that adolescence could be a confusing time. The following week he seemed more certain that he was attracted to boys, the week after he thought he may be pansexual, which is when a person is attracted to others because of their personality (you would hope that was a major factor anyway) and then the next week he had decided he was bisexual. He stayed back for a couple of weeks after that making small talk about Brexit again, but I got the impression that something was still bothering him. A week later he was there again, 'Can I talk to you please after the lesson?' he asked as usual. He knew the answer was always yes, as it was lunchtime and I usually lost my 40-minute lunch 'break' talking to students anyway. (Ah! Those were the days! We currently have 25 minutes at the most) His face was looking even more serious than usual this week. He made sure the door was closed, and then he let it all flood out. He really wanted to be gay, bisexual or even pansexual but after a great deal of reflection and soul searching he had come to the disappointing conclusion that he was straight, and he needed to come out. The dismay was almost too much for him to bear.

Disclosures from students when talking about various topics in PSHE comes with the territory and is to be expected. All our concerns were reported on a secure online programme which alerted the SLT and safeguarding officers who would decide what to do next. Occasionally a topic would cause a flurry of disclosures and my SLT would jokingly tell me to stop teaching whatever it was as their emails were clogged up with my reports. Over the years some of these disclosures have been distressing to hear and like the previous school cohort, many of the students at this school also had difficult back stories.

Teaching PSHE gave me an excellent opportunity to be able to teach young people directly about well-being and mental health and try to help them to increase their resilience. I regularly told them they were amazing for being as strong as they were and tried to empower them to understand the consequences of the choices they were making. I felt so lucky that I was in a position where I could assess what the students needed to know and devise a curriculum which was tailored for them. In a school where some, but not all students leave with GCSEs we have the responsibility to teach them all how to survive and thrive in real life.

I feel passionately that all schools could play a more useful role in preparing young people for adulthood. We allow students to leave school not knowing about finances, how to read a bank statement, make a budget, know the difference between a credit and a debit card or understand the importance of their credit score. Many mainstream students do not know what the signs are that a relationship is becoming abusive or even what to do if their condom bursts and they end up in a pickle.

We also have a generation who do not properly understand the importance of nutrition and how what they eat affects their mood and their physical health, with cheap food causing obesity, illness and even malnutrition. I think we have a duty to inform students about the effects of alcohol and drugs so that they can make informed choices- it's not our job to preach or pretend that we are perfect, but give young people the information they need about consequences and choices so that when they make their own decisions they do so with some knowledge.

Other topics included sexual exploitation, peer pressure, human rights, the legal system, politics, media, consumer rights, bullying, cyber safety, knife crime, dental hygiene, general hygiene, tax, renting, mortgages, gambling and many others. During every one-hour lesson I had with each class, I tried my best to engage them with the topic, and found news reports, videos and the newest resources which meant a continual reworking of schemes of work to keep everything fresh and meaningful.

I strongly believe that PSHE should be taken more seriously in mainstream education. Often it is given a cursory half hour during form time, often teachers are irritated that they have the responsibility for it and I think that this really needs to change. I was once at a conference with hundreds of delegates when somebody said that in their opinion PSHE wasn't important as there is no formal qualification at the end of it. I hate public speaking but I was trembling with anger and had to raise my hand to point out that certificates shouldn't be the end goal of education. Surely we are there to give young people the information and support they need to be able to live independently, safely and happily, and contribute to society, for the rest of their lives? I did point out that there are certificates available, if that's your main aim, but it just seems very short sighted to me.

Chapter 21 Corona

J ust when things were ticking along as steadily as they ever do in life, along came the corona virus. Back in early March 2020 when we were first hearing about it, one student appeared from her taxi wearing a mask. This student often wore strange things on her head- usually a rainbow coloured sparkly unicorn headband, sometimes a massive and alarming painted cardboard dog head (with matching paws) which she had crafted at home. She was widely ridiculed for the face mask and asked not to wear it in school. How things have changed since then.

None of us could have ever imagined what the next year would look like. For those people who believe the tabloids and think that all schools closed for a year and all teachers and support staff lay in the bath and drank gin, I am sorry but this wasn't the case. It was a very challenging year in teaching, and continues to be difficult. I think I have painted a fairly clear picture of what the reality of teaching is- groups of young people are never predictable or easy to manage. Emotionally it is draining, there are times when it makes you go home and cry, or drink too much, or search the job ads. The paperwork is huge and has to be done at weekends as there is no time during the week to do anything other than deal with day-to-day teaching and planning, emails and phonecalls, sorting out practical issues and supporting students (or colleagues) with emotional distress, as well as a million other things which assault you from the moment you step into the building.

If home schooling is hard, this is a tiny, fun-sized snapshot of teaching. It requires energy, patience and forward planning to engage a whole class of students with different needs. The preparation of every lesson takes roughly the same amount of time as it does to teach it, so multiply that by 6 lessons every day, relentlessly, with no proper break during the day and you can maybe imagine how it is. Draining. And that is just the teaching part- there are meetings to attend, training to do, forms and reports to fill in, phone calls to make, child protection issues to action, emails to chase up, policies to update. We stumble towards the next teaching break, knowing that at least there will be a little space, some non-contact time when we can catch up with paperwork. Paperwork has taken over teaching.

We also have to juggle looking after our own children, or other family members, who always seem to take second place to the demands of the job. In those half term breaks most of the time is spent doing schoolwork, some time is spent cleaning things that have been neglected all term, and some time is spent taking people to dental or medical appointments that couldn't be made during work time. If you are massively organised, you might get a haircut yourself- but that requires spare energy. Every teacher I know works through the half terms and even in the summer we still have accreditation work to sort out, schemes to plan and new classes to prepare for. The main perk of teaching isn't the holidays anyway, they are needed for survival. The main perk is the buzz you get from knowing that you have made a difference, whether that is seeing progress or achievement or helping with advice or reassurance. It is the interaction you have with the students and the laughter that you share with colleagues which makes the job worth doing. If you take that personal interaction away, which is what happens when face to face teaching stops, you are just left with paperwork, and that's not the same job.

In the first lockdown there were still a high number of children with EHCP plans attending schools, and this has continued throughout the pandemic. All students with EHCs were considered 'vulnerable' so this made safety decisions and organisation very hard for those people involved at a school management level. We were providing online learning and sending out work packs, staff working in rotas to support 'bubbles'. All students were contacted at least once a week, especially those students known to be in difficult home environments. From home we were tasked with rewriting schemes of work, providing lesson plans for every lesson for every class for the whole year. This was intended as a two-year project, but in lock down we were expected to have it well underway. Throughout the good weather we slogged on, linking lessons to Right Respecting schools articles, Spiritual, Moral, Social and Cultural links, British Values, Preparation for Adulthood and 'Character Education'- that last one was my fault. I had an idea we could link all those aspects of personal development which aren't assessed formally and developed a programme designed to measure them, which linked in to interventions and behaviour reports. It took months, but after it was all completed I felt happy that if anything happened to me, someone could step in and have a fairly decent scheme of work to follow. What a legacy to leave the world. All my stuff was linked to the PSHE Association programmes of study and the national curriculum citizenship units and was in line with the legal changes which had come into force about relationship and sex education. If that sound a bit dull, it was, but hand on heart I worked long hours, knowing I was lucky to still have a job and wanting to prove I was working as hard as possible.

When lockdown was eased and schools went back fully it was a relief to everyone, and we soon got back into the usual routines. I was teaching in 20 different bubbles, amounting to 230 students each week. The government propaganda made out that bubbles were invincible, impenetrable and super safe, with no mixing or bursting at all. Of course this would have been ideal, but it was impractical in secondary settings. In primary it is more feasible to stay together with the class teacher and steady support staff, but in secondary school, students obviously need specialist teachers. Social distancing in schools is another misnomer. Unless every school extended its school buildings and doubled or trebled the space available, students cannot keep a meter or two meters apart. Nothing has physically changed in schools, and most are crowded, so the gap between students is usually exactly as it was pre pandemic, and that's often just a few inches away from each other. As the government advice stood, we were not to wear masks in the classroom but must wear them in the corridors. My school arranged it so that students remained in their form rooms for most of the time and staff went and visited them there to teach. This reduced the amount of traffic in the corridors, which was an excellent idea. However, it meant that we would arrive at work, put our masks on to walk down an empty corridor and remove them in a classroom where there were 3 or 4 other members of staff and up to 15 students, all not socially distanced. If anybody needed to use the toilet during a lesson, they would put their mask on, go back out into the empty corridor, visit the toilet and remove the mask again when they got back in the company of their classmates and teachers.

The government guidelines made little sense. Many of our students suffered from anxiety and ASC, many of these students understood about the risks of the virus, had been listening to the news, and had taken on board advice about handwashing, social distancing and masks. Therefore, the situation they found themselves in at school actually made their anxiety worse, as they knew what we had all been told to do and yet it somehow didn't apply in school. They wore masks on their taxi and then took them off in the classroom. Many people with autism are perfectly intelligent, they just have a different way of thinking, which is sometimes more rigid, so to apply rules in one place and not in another was confusing and stressful to them. The media, however, did not acknowledge this- no studies have been done as far as I know to gauge how many young people felt this way. I know that many staff were also uncomfortable as levels of cases started to rise again and the 'second lockdown' was imposed after the October half term everywhere it seemed, except schools.

Many staff were on the vulnerable list or had vulnerable or clinically extremely vulnerable loved ones at home (me included). We went to work each day, knowing cases and death numbers were rising, all of us knew somebody who had died, but we wore no PPE, had no perspex screens to protect us, no limits on numbers in each room and no social distancing. There were arbitrary rules elsewhere in the school, the conference rooms, staff room and office were regarded as more 'communal' so restrictions were enforced about social distancing and numbers. We had staff members becoming ill and pupils off sick, many of whom refused to take a test. If we suspected a student had symptoms, it was like that scene from Monsters Inc where the anti-contamination officers zoom in and remove the offending monster. If a member of a class bubble tested positive the whole bubble was closed down, we had to stay in our form room and wait there until the very last student had been collected and then the room was deep cleaned. It felt a bit like continuing to play in the orchestra on the deck of the Titanic as it started to sink.

Our students were a mixed bunch, some followed the rules, such as they were, while others deliberately coughed, breathed or spat at others because it guaranteed a dramatic reaction. A small number of students continued to need occasional physical interventions, and when somebody is in a position of danger and needs restraining there is no time to stop and put on a mask or visor. PMLD students continued to need intimate personal care, and supporting most students, especially SLD or visually impaired students required close 1:1 support- impossible at a one or two-meter distance. All the students needed us all to work closely with them and that couldn't happen from an imaginary box, taped off at the front of the classroom. I know of no teachers who managed to remain inside their box, and the support staff didn't even have a box, an oversight by the government that helped them to feel even less valued.

To practice the skills we needed in order to do remote teaching we were encouraged to have a 'dummy run' in the autumn term (appropriate wording there) . My laptop would randomly choose whether to join in these attempts- sometimes it would connect to zoom but have no camera, sometimes it didn't mind Teams but would have no sound. It would never work as it should and it exasperated our usually calm and unflappable ICT support man. I tried teaching from my cupboard, feeling the sinister presence of the thing in the filing cabinet and the twin hairy freak dolls watching me from the darkness. My class were in the classroom, watching the whiteboard- I would appear momentarily in my cupboard amongst a stash of tampax and condoms before the connection would fail and we would have to rethink. We decided it would be more realistic to emulate the lockdown situation and attempt to connect the class individually on laptops. There were three of us staff and 14 students- the rest of that lesson was spent helping the students to remember their passwords and trying to log on. Eventually I was given a different laptop, but unfortunately not in time to have another practice.

Meanwhile, all the external agencies who supported us in normal circumstances seemed to shut down and work from home, including psychology services, occupational health, physio, speech therapy, CAMHs and many more. Meetings and training all went virtual, everyone had risk assessed us and decided they would keep away. In the extremely rare event they did attend the school in person, they would ring from the carpark for an update on the plague situation and expect to be escorted, at a distance, to a sterile room where they would meet, at a distance with one un-sneezing non-coughing, clean looking student wearing a mask. We had no non-essential external visitors, volunteers or student teachers, even union reps were keeping themselves safely out of schools and we could not take the students off site. We were all exhausted by the end of term and had never been so ready for a break. We all knew the risks we were putting ourselves and our families under, and with no PPE and no so-

cial distancing it felt like only a matter of time before we became sick.

Chapter 22 Lockdown 2 (not counting the pointless one in October)

After Christmas and during the lead up to schools opening for the spring term there were regularly in excess of 50,000 new corona virus cases reported each day, and some of the unions were encouraging staff to invoke their right to a safe working environment under section 44 of the Employment Act 1996. There were rumours that if staff did this they could be sacked, but the idea of putting their families at risk, and risking the lives of students and colleagues meant that many felt they had an impossible choice. Schools were open on the Monday after the Christmas break, but were told on the Monday night by the Department for Education that all schools would be closed to most pupils from the following day. Lessons were to go 'live' from the Wednesday, giving us very little time to set up lists of students for whom school would be open, work out which students would need paper copies of work packs posting out, and to organise all the information parents would need. We had INSET training on the Monday and the Tuesday and I worked late into the evenings both nights trying to organise live lessons, practicing the technical bits like screen sharing and uploading worksheets, and then adapting work to accommodate students who had no access to online learning.

All those schemes of work I had spent months writing in the summer needed adapting or completely abandoning for virtual 'live' lessons. The interactive activity parts of each lesson were impossible to do through a computer, and many students were trying to access lessons through ipads and phones. It was a very steep learning curve.

That first week was really difficult, negotiating around Microsoft Teams was a nightmare, and I ended up sending all my lesson invitations to a neighbouring school by accident. The really weird thing was that some people (random adults included) seemed happy to accept them. It took most of the week to sort this out, booking them through each team page or through the calendar did different things to the lists of attendees and I am still not sure how or why. That first day, every moment between attempting live lessons was spent on the phone to the lovely long suffering ICT technician or to exasperated parents trying to explain how to log on. Each lesson took at least two hours to prepare, worksheets needed adapting and uploading, some lessons were recorded in advance but it was soon clear that this was even more stressful than delivering the lesson live.

Without any feedback, which is what teaching is all

about, it is impossible to know if you are having any impact and whether any learning has happened. Most of the live lessons were recorded anyway, which was handy for students who were unable to log on at the time, or who found a particular part of the lesson hilarious and wanted to watch it over and over again. There were so many of these moments- if anyone had time to compile them into an out-takes video it would have top trumped The Tiger King for lock down viewing.

My ineptitude continued once a lesson was set up- in some lessons the class were somehow already there before me. In others I was given no notification that people were in the lobby waiting. The powerpoints I wanted to use vanished, the videos had no sound. Sometimes, I would share my screen with the students and then be unable to navigate my way back to the lesson for an embarrassingly long time. To add to the stress, it was often unclear who else was attending online lessons from the students' homes. One of my students had the whole family there, three generations, plus the dog, all lined up and squashed together on the sofa waiting for action. Sometimes they would forget to mute themselves and the class could overhear personal conversations or heated arguments. At other times, mum, dad or carer could be overheard supplying the answers to quiz questions or sniggering at technical issues. Some enthusiastic parents would actually take part in the whole lesson in place of their child, who was nowhere to be seen, and this was very odd. This reportedly happened a number of times in PE, when parents would be all kitted out in sportswear, bravely star jumping on behalf of their children. They were blissfully unaware that the camera angle created by a device perched on a knee high coffee table made it difficult for the staff to concentrate fully on the lesson and remain professional.

It was worse than being observed by OFSTED as there were so many variables and so much potential for it all to go wrong. I taught four lessons one day with my hairy black chihuahua sitting on the back of the sofa behind me with a poo tangled up in his fluffy bum hair. On another occasion my husband decided to do some prolonged, pointless and intermittent drilling in the cellar directly beneath me which rendered my English lesson completely inaudible. Stuff was obviously happening in every household though- so I felt a little better about these blips. I thought I'd overstepped the mark one day when I noted the disappearance of a massive bottle of wine (which had replaced a big bottle of gin) which usually featured as a backdrop for one of my students. 'It's in the fridge!' shouted an irritated mother when I joked about it. The next time there were two large cartons of fresh orange juice in its place. I waited for a phone call from management to remind me there were probably protocols about commenting on parental alcohol consumption (as if I was in any position to comment).

It wasn't great for my self-esteem having to spend all day staring at myself on a screen, I looked like a tired and crazy old man, although I was marginally better looking in the kitchen than the living room. The turnout for the online lessons was quite good, but I suspected that most students were attending to laugh at my ICT abilities or to make me into an amusing meme to share later on social media. One of the staff reminded us that their head had already been pasted onto the body of a porn star a few years earlier, so we knew that they had the skills. Keeping behaviour under control in a virtual classroom was also a steep learning curve. For some unfathomable reason if we were watching a video or a powerpoint I could not see the 'group chat' or message board, where students could type messages to each other in real time. This meant that there could potentially be all kinds of shenanigans going on which I was oblivious to until after the lesson. Some problems arose because students had misspelled their comments in the chat or predictive text had interfered and it had accidentally caused offence to somebody else or to their parent. These mixed up text arguments soon escalated and took a bit of calming down. I found a photo of a Land Rover had been uploaded during one lesson on cyber bullying, and ironically in another on gaming addiction students were encouraging each other to leave the lesson and play Roblox instead.

There were only really a couple of lessons which were likely to go haywire from a behavioural point of view so I nipped them in the bud from the start. I figured out how to mute the students but the unwanted side effect of this was that it muted any support staff too. Much of the learning in PSHE happens through discussion work, so during these lessons it was mainly me discussing different viewpoints with myself. I tried releasing the mute function at the end of one lesson, but my suspicions were proved right and one of them managed to sneak in a comment about me being a useless babyboomer with no understanding of ICT. The ICT part was true, but I was very offended by the babyboomer comment- he had misjudged my age by about 30 years, although to be fair the whole 'live' virtual teaching thing had definitely aged me by at least 25. After that I tightened the reins again and for the next lesson with this group I muted everyone, including myself. I was unaware of this until afterwards, when one of the support staff sent me a message. 'Did you know we couldn't hear you for the whole lesson?' they asked.

Keeping tabs on work returned was equally tricky. Some students were doing none and not engaging online either. School staff kept in regular contact with these students and sent out paper copies in the hope that they would at least try to keep up. Others produced an amazing amount of work, far more than we expected. Some kept it all at home and delivered it on their return, in one massive bundle. Others emailed photographs of it and some uploaded it to Teams, occasionally sending it to the wrong teacher or subject area. We were so proud of the effort they put in, engagement with live lessons was much better than we expected, and generally staff felt that this second lockdown had been more successful than the first, despite all the teething troubles. Working from home was full on, I had imagined I would be able to pop in a sneaky load of washing or walk the dog at lunchtime but this just didn't happen.

Time was now measured differently, each day was now a series of numbers and letters depending on the year group I was teaching and the initial of the form tutor attached to that group, so Thursday might be 8D, 10M, 8D, 7M and 9F. I needed to be online and available all day every day. Between lessons there might be no gap, so all the powerpoints, video links and worksheets needed to be ready and documents lined up so as to avoid too many technical issues. If there was a gap between lessons, I would be responding to emails from students or parents and giving feedback on work. I had previously felt a little jealous of people who sat in front of a computer all day, safely away from the unpredictability and potential danger of the 'front line'. Now I felt differently.. it was tedious staring at a screen all day. My eyesight went weird, my shoulders ached, and I have already mentioned the impact on my wellbeing of having to see my own aging face looking back at me constantly. I missed the good bits about teaching, missed the relationships I had with the students, and the friendship of colleagues. The 'live' lessons were no substitute, it rendered the colourful inexplicable wholeness of the job into a very black and white soulless one-dimensional transaction.

All the time the media were telling the world that schools were closed and teachers were off, again. The truth was so different- most (if not all) schools, ours included, had never shut. We had a rota of support staff working tirelessly with bubbles of students in classrooms, others doing home visits to support families and check on students known to be in difficult domestic circumstances, and teams producing and delivering workpacks for students without IT at home. Nobody was 'off'. For management, the situation was like an on-going nightmare, made worse by the volumes of DFE guidance which actually said very little or changed without any warning. It was up to management to read through the entire document each time it was updated, as the changes were not highlighted Our school managed the situation well, and took their responsibilities to protect students and staff seriously.

The media also spewed out a daily stream of negativity about our young people, the 'lost generation' who were all suffering mental health issues and would have their life chances obliterated by the pandemic. This has helped nobody. Some of our anxious ASC students thrived during the second lockdown, either from the reduced stress of withdrawing socially, or from being in school but having a much higher staffing ratio. The job of home schooling is undoubtedly very difficult but adding more and more pressure on to parents makes them feel resentful and stressed. As an experienced teacher I found home schooling during the first lockdown very tedious. Home is meant to be a safe place where people can relax and feel happy. If you change the rules and try to turn it into a school, it isn't going to be easy. What would have been more helpful would have been messages of support from the government and the media- they could have told the nation they were proud of the dedicated and determined efforts made by schools and the amazing resilience shown by our young people. That might have helped to alleviate some of the mental health crisis post lockdown.

Chapter 23   Return to Normal-Ish

"**W**hat number is it outside?" a boy randomly asked me at the end of a lesson. He was looking at me with one of his eyes, but the other was gazing behind me, which was distracting. "I'm not sure" I replied, "What number would you like it to be?" I was stalling, not sure where the conversation was heading. I find that if you keep talking, eventually you can usually work out what is going on.

"I don't know" he admitted. "But last night it was 7, AND I WAS OUT IN MY PANTS!" he bellowed at me, then he laughed gleefully and ran away.

I had missed conversations like this.

In another classroom, the staff were trying to write down what each student wanted for their lunch that day. This was always a lengthy and surprisingly difficult job. It seemed to involve reading the list of options to each of the dozen or so students individually and repeating the question, "Do you want chips or jacket?" an amazing number of times. One of the students was a refugee from Syria, who had joined the school a year earlier. He had come with no spoken English but had made fantastic progress, however there were still a number of our strange customs which he found confusing. He was tolerant and smiled encouragingly at the staff while they explained for the tenth time that morning that it was a choice of fish fingers or curry. He looked confused. "FISH FINGERS" the staff member said more loudly, as many of us do when faced with a language barrier. He politely shrugged and asked what that meant. "FINGERS" was the reply (and there was a helpful fluttering of the hand) "MADE OF FISH" The boy looked horrified and chose the curry.

The following week I walked in during the same routine. This week however, there was a menu change, and I heard the member of staff shouting helpfully to the Syrian boy "FISHCAKES" and a little while later "WELL, THEY'RE CAKES.... MADE OF FISH" He just looked at her as though to say, 'You people are so weird' and chose the alternative.

Later the same day, one of our more rebellious students had made the wrong choice, telling his teacher exactly what he'd thought of them and their lesson and so was having a little time out in the 'small group room'. Often the students would be offered the space to calm down and would then return to lessons. Usually, a staff member would spend time talking with them to work out what had triggered the behaviour and talk through alternative ways of dealing with the issue. On this occasion, the student had decided to have some 'me time', to relax across the comfortable and newly re padded bench seat, chill out, catch up on social media, (he had chosen to keep hold of his phone- he was a popular guy in the outside world) and put his feet up. Then, as if the flouting of the phone rules wasn't bad enough, he reached into his coat pocket, pulled out a packet of fags and a lighter and casually lit up. It did surprise the staff, but it was not a new habit- his mother had been enabling him to self soothe with nicotine since he was in primary school, and he found the tediousness of our school rules made him want to smoke even more.

At the end of a long day I was escorting some of my students to their taxi feeling absolutely shattered. I saw a bright yellow lighter on the floor and thought 'Oh it looks like someone has stood on that' but didn't think anything more. Later, when a more conscious staff member found it and there was a discussion, I admitted I'd seen it earlier, but my brain had been unable to process it. This happens more than it should. The continual bombardment to the brain by requests and demands from above, (by which I mean management/ government rather than God) and the relentless and bizarre questions from the students eventually fries the mind.

The following day I sat down at my computer,

in my classroom, and noticed that a load of stationery items including a ruler, rubber and whiteboard marker as well as more miscellaneous things such as a box of tissues had all been glued to the wall. My first thought was that the feeble school glue had done a surprisingly good job considering it usually struggled to deal with every day paper-to-paper situations. On closer inspection I could see that the stuff had been squashed in handfuls against the wall and the items had been forced into it- still impressive. The reasons behind it were a mystery, and still are. The student who normally sits next to me appeared, cast me a guilty sideways look and immediately set about unsticking everything, armed with a bunch of damp paper towels. We all know that damp paper towels are the answer to everything from a bruise to a haemorrhage and he managed surprisingly well. No explanation was ever offered but now when I can't find a board pen I tend to look at the walls just incase they have been reglued there.

I was reminded of a story told to me by an old friend, who had ended up having to transport three girls to hospital after they had sealed their friendship with super glue. Their hands needed to be medically unstuck and the seatbelt arrangements on the way there hadn't been easy.

One of our students was under surveillance for secret eating. Her weight was causing her health problems and there was social work support to try to limit the number of kebabs at home. She was permitted only one pudding a week and this was causing some behavioural issues, including assaulting a member of the kitchen staff with a piece of chocolate cake when she tried to enforce the rules. The student would attempt stealth break ins to the dining room and would try to steal food like a well-built hungry ninja. We had all been warned to be on high alert.

Our group emails are often littered with peculiar requests like this. 'Ignore X, they need to wear flippers today' 'Don't comment to Y, they accidentally left the fake tan on too long' etc. On another occasion we were told not to tell this particular student off because she had come to school in cycling shorts (to allow air flow), and she had teamed them with a pair of grubby, slip-on fluffy slippers. One day I decided to leave my lunch in the car, just so that I would get some of my 25 minutes without students asking me what was in my sandwiches, when I saw her. She made such a striking picture of misery. She was standing on the yard with her back to me, her forehead pressed against the external door, her shoulders drooped and hopeless, just waiting for the doors to open and for somebody to let her in for dinner.

Another boy had struggled with similar issues. One day, we found that his mother had rammed 12 generous pieces of corned beef pie into a plastic car-rier bag and squashed it into his rucksack. When tactfully questioned, he said that she had given it to him for morning break in case he was peckish. No amount of healthy eating education in school can fight against the irresistibility of home-made corned beef pie or nightly kebabs with extra chips.

These are just moments from a couple of days of post lockdown school life, and I love it, we are al-most back to the way things were. Despite the blip in January and February and the fact that masks are still worn, schools have been operating fairly normally. Lateral flow testing has been set up and some students are still choosing to test at school. In unofficial polls of our class there are maybe 30% of other students also testing at home. However, there is still a reluctance to return to the premises from many of the outside agencies who normally support students. Despite the close conditions that teachers and support staff have been working in for months, some organisations or departments still request magical 'covid free' rooms which can ac-commodate a 2-meter space around them and ask that students wear masks for the duration of their visit. It seems a very odd disparity of working con-ditions.

The TV reports that office workers are slowly re-turning to their offices, while some are choosing to continue to work from home. Overall, so far, we have been lucky. We have had a number of staff and students who have caught covid and a few who have been very poorly, but it could have been so much worse and we can only hope that the Delta variant does not become a bigger problem. A worrying health risk at our workplace seems to be heart attacks. We have had four staff members suffer in the last two years, one of whom sadly died.

My mission, currently, is to try to improve staff and student wellbeing, and since returning to work I have gathered together a band of like minded colleagues who are also dedicated to trying to change things for the better. Statistically, across the UK, 1/3 of teachers leave the job within 5 years, numbers which are similar for nurses. Pre pandemic 57% of teachers were thinking about leaving the job so I wonder what the numbers are like now. As this book has mentioned several times, the teaching part of a teacher's role is only a fraction of what needs to be done... schools educate young people but also do so much more than that. New teachers are generally, blissfully unprepared for the total emotional and social immersion of the job. The 'Every Child Matters' initiative brought in in 2003 was shelved by the conservative coalition in 2010 but continues to be the philosophy at the heart of most of the people I know who work in education. I have found over the last 25 years that the role has broadened considerably, and unless we can all move to a position where wellbeing is supported first, we will not succeed to educate. I have been so glad to watch what appears to be a new mental health revolution unfolding but find it ironic at the same time that that the media and government have contributed to the problem by continuing to tell everyone that they are doomed, failing or lost.

With the current generation of students, post lockdown, we are also competing, perhaps more than ever before, with a never-ending and addictive stream of memes, social media, and gaming choices. The time some of them have spent gaming during lockdown has made even harder to engage them in lessons. 'Hooking' students into a lesson when their attention span has decreased and difficulties in interacting with people has increased, requires enormous effort. In each lesson we need to draw on a number of different strategies and types of media through which to engage and entertain them, video clips, quizzes, drawing, discussion, games, role pay, or whatever works for each student, plus, of course, written work (we always need evidence for the system to scrutinise!) As we enter the classroom, fully prepared with all our differentiated resources, we read the room, make a mental note of the atmosphere, mood, facial expressions, and body language of the class. We adapt the pattern of the lesson according to what is going on and continue to do that all the way through. We must gauge how to phrase questions and how to respond, who needs encouragement and who might go off track. We need to figure out whether each student has understood a concept and back track if necessary. Continually assessing mood and learning, whether the pace is too quick or too slow, whether a change of delivery is needed.

We are acting most of the time- pretending we aren't stressed by all these decisions, pretending that a palpable change in atmosphere is going to be fine, we can handle it if tables are tipped, or chairs thrown. Despite the inevitable burst of adrenalin, we maintain a calm expression and show no signs of surprise if a string of obscenities or insults is thrown at us, we do not take it personally and the next time we meet that student we must pretend it never happened. Everything usually runs smoothly, but only because of the skills of the staff and their ability to respond in the right way to each individual student. It's challenging work and changing audiences so frequently is exhausting- I imagine what it must be like to be a stand-up comedian doing a difficult tour of gigs and can sympathise. To survive you must be able to handle any hecklers, keep smiling and carry on. I am so lucky to work with the support staff that I have, particularly in my current class. We keep eachother going because we keep eachother laughing.

I also agree with Harold Edgerton, who pointed out in the 1950's "The trick to education is to teach in such a way that people only find out they're learning when it's too late". The challenge is to revive the love of learning that we are born with, not kill it with SATS, pen licences and tedious grammar exercises. Let's hope that the 'silver lining' of the corona virus is that we look again at how we educate our young people and have a reshuffling of priorities.

I feel lucky to have had such a wide range of experience in my career, from Cumbria to Convent, mainstream primary to SEND secondary and I have taught some of the most challenging and fantastic young people in the northeast. I have learned so much from so many awe inspiring people, family, friends, colleagues and of course my students. The traumatic or negative experiences have made me a better, kinder person and I am certainly stronger and more resilient.

We all have a story, one of my very gifted students told me recently that there is even a special word for it, 'prosopography'. This collection of ramblings has been just a few bits of mine, every day stuff from a slightly odd, greying, middle aged teacher and mum of four.

I don't regret the choices I have made, but I do acknowledge with admiration and horror that 'Baby Spice' is only a few years younger than me. I have now started to use sun cream as a moisturiser, because maybe, if I'd chosen a different career, I would look less 'care worn', although I have probably never looked as young as Baby Spice, even as a baby.

I am tired, sometimes even exhausted, but not too tired to reflect, look back from this point and laugh. We all get it wrong sometimes, we all carry pain from things that have happened in the past, but I believe the main thing is to keep plodding on, giving love and helping others as we go, being the best versions of ourselves that we can be. 'Love is what love does' is my mum's mantra, and as my cheerful, food loving grandma used to say;

'Cast your bread upon the water and it comes back buttered.'

Even if it ends up soggy and some of it sinks.

That Book Written by a Teacher
My Bizarre descent into Exhaustion

Thank you for reading this page, and thank you again if you made it through the whole book.

Printed in Great Britain
by Amazon